The Memoirs of Bing Devine

Stealing Lou Brock and Other Winning Moves by a Master GM

Bing Devine
with
Tom Wheatley

Sports Publishing L.L.C.
www.sportspublishingllc.com

Director of production: Susan M. Moyer
Project manager: Jim Henehan
Dust jacket design: Kenneth J. O'Brien
Developmental editor: Doug Hoepker
Copy editor: Cindy McNew
Photo editor: Erin Linden-Levy

ISBN: 1-58261-763-5

Printed in the United States of America

Sports Publishing L.L.C.
www.sportspublishingllc.com

To Mary and the girls—Joanne, Janice and Jane:

Thanks for putting up with my many absences, for your welcome opinions and criticisms, and for your love and support through difficult times. Of all my teams, you've been the best.

To my grandchildren—Devin, Russell, Zachary, Edwin, Bennett, Geoff, Scott and Alex—and great-grandchildren Joe and Molly:

I love you all, and my life would have been meaningless without you.

Contents

Foreword

I'm not sure when I first met Bing Devine. I do know he's one of the absolute best baseball men I've ever met.

I've been a baseball junkie all my life, ever since I saw my first Cardinals game in 1946. I loved Sportsman's Park. I still hate that they tore it down.

I'm involved with the Kansas City Royals now, but for most of my life it was only the Cardinals. So I knew of Bing when he was general manager, the talent that he is, and the job that he does.

One of the reasons I've been involved in baseball was Bing's counseling. I've been in retail advertising all my life, and eventually I thought it might be fun to own a baseball team. I had no idea if that was a ridiculous idea or if it had any merit.

So I called Bing and asked if he could put together a group of people to answer some questions about whether it was practical for me to get involved.

Bing set up a luncheon in St. Louis. He got Stan Musial and Bob Broeg and some other people who would be resources for me to talk to. They all had different perspectives. It was very helpful to me.

And ultimately, based on that luncheon and subsequent discussions with Bing, I decided I did want to get into baseball.

About those discussions, one of the things I most enjoyed was going to a baseball game with Bing. First of all, he had great seats! It was just fun watching the game with him and hearing him talk about what was happening. And I learned an awful lot from him.

The first team that I thought about acquiring was the Houston Astros. I remember Bing counseling me about that. But I live in Arkansas, and I didn't care about the Astros the way I did about the Cardinals and the Royals. I didn't have a connection like that with Houston.

Then a friend of mine who owned the Royals, Ewing Kaufman, was ill and wanted to sell the team. And Bing counseled me on buying the Royals.

With Bing, I've always been able to pick up the phone and ask for his opinions on things. I've asked him about players and managers and different talent for our club. And I still like to keep in touch because I value his knowledge about baseball. He's like an encyclopedia.

One thing I've found is that people in baseball have tremendous respect for Bing. I'm always amazed by how many people admire him.

Someone who really admires Bing is Joe Torre. When Joe comes to Kansas City with the Yankees, he always asks me about Bing and about how he's doing.

You find that all over baseball—that kind of respect for Bing Devine.

Through the years, he's had some things happen to him that were unfair. He always lets it go and moves on. Bing's always taken the high road. That's the best way to do it. You and I would just raise hell and make a big issue out of it.

I like Bing's approach. I can't do it, but I like it!

So I am really excited that he wrote this book. Now I can finally see how he's done it all these years.

—*David Glass*
Owner and Chief Executive Officer, Kansas City Royals
Chairman of the Executive Committee, Wal-Mart Stores

Acknowledgments

I've been fortunate and privileged to work with a number of talented men and women in my 65 years in professional sports. You'll meet many of them in this book. But I'd like to give special mention to the following.

Dick Meyer, my mentor in every phase of life.

Mr. August A. Busch Jr., for taking a chance on me—not once, but twice.

Al Fleishman, the great public relations man, who always led me down the right trails.

The Cardinals' owners, in particular Drew Baur, Bill DeWitt Jr. and Fred Hanser, for keeping baseball strong in St. Louis—and for thinking I have something left.

David Glass, a born Cardinals fan who now roots for the Royals, for our compelling conversations on baseball—and for his flattering foreword to this book.

Judy Barada, Lou Brock, Bob Broeg, Bob Harlan, Whitey Herzog, Walt Jocketty, Marty Marion, Stan Musial, Red Schoendienst, Mike Shannon and Lee Thomas, for sharing their wonderful memories of our work together in these pages.

Dr. Stan London, without whose advice and friendship I'd be lost.

Dan Rosen and Jim Bogart, my friends on the St. Louis Sports Commission, whose encouragement made this book happen.

All the members of the media, whose fair coverage kept me on my toes throughout the years.

And finally, thanks to the fans everywhere who have rooted for teams that I've worked for—especially the knowledgeable and passionate baseball fans of St. Louis, who have made it all worthwhile.

Chapter 1

General Rules for a General Manager

Stealing Lou Brock

When we made the deal for Lou Brock in 1964, we were playing in Los Angeles on the 14th of June. The trading deadline then was June 15, not the end of July, as it is now.

We had indicated our interest in Brock to the Cubs for a long time. We had talked to them about it during the winter, and we had talked about a Brock deal during the season. But John Holland, the Cubs' general manager, always rejected it. He'd say, "We're not going to deal him."

But when we were in Los Angeles the day before the deadline, I was making the rounds by phone from Dodger Stadium, calling the other general managers to see if we could do anything to improve the Cardinals. And when I called John Holland this time, he said, "If you're still interested, we might have to move Brock."

I said, "For what?"

He said, "We need a pitcher. You gave me a list of players when we talked before, and we'll take a pitcher off that list. We'll take Broglio."

Ernie Broglio was one of our top starting pitchers. He had won 18 games the year before. I told Holland, "I'll have to check with my manager."

Our manager was Johnny Keane. I didn't get a chance to talk to him until after the game, when we were on the plane flying to Houston. I can remember this so clearly. I told Johnny we had a chance to get Brock for Broglio, and he said, "What are we waiting for?"

Remember, there were no cell phones then. I told him, "I'll call as soon as we land and I can get to a pay phone."

Closing the Deal

I really had to make two calls when we landed in Houston. Our owner, Gussie Busch, always said that the last thing he wanted was to read about a trade in the paper. So first I reached Dick Meyer by phone. He was a vice president and the number one assistant to Mr. Busch at Anheuser-Busch.

Talking to Dick Meyer was like talking to Mr. Busch, and Dick didn't have any problems with the trade. I called Holland back and told him we were ready to make the deal. We both put two other players in there—Bobby Shantz and Doug Clemens from the Cards and Jack Spring and Paul Toth from the Cubs—and that was it.

Our first game with Brock in Houston, I was in a box seat down behind the Cardinals' dugout. I was with Art Routzong, my right-hand man, and we kept hearing this fan in the stands hollering, "Brock for Broglio? Who'd make that deal?"

He didn't know who I was. He was just being funny. And he kept yelling that.

Brock played that night. He didn't do anything bad, but he didn't do anything good.

When the game was over, and we were walking out, I said to Art, tongue in cheek, "Brock for Broglio? Who in the world could make that deal?"

Not the People's Choice

Most of the fans and media in St. Louis didn't think much of Brock for Broglio.

Broglio had won 20 games for us in 1960 before winning those 18 games in '63. But in '64, he was 3-5 for us in 11 games when we made the trade.

Brock had been a regular for the Cubs for two years. He hit .263 in '62 and .258 in '63, and he stole only 16 bases the first year, when Maury Wills led the league with 104, and just 24 the next year.

And Brock wasn't a really good outfielder. He had trouble playing in Wrigley Field. Occasionally, he'd throw a ball over home plate and into the stands.

For a player who could run, he also struck out a lot. Most people don't realize that. If he were a better contact hitter, how many more stolen bases would he have had? If he'd been on base more, he'd have had so many more chances to run. That's what amazes me.

Even given all these factors, we really liked his potential. But that's why the Cubs were willing to move him. Plus they needed a pitcher.

As it turned out, Broglio went 4-7 after he went over to the Cubs. And in '65, he went 1-6 and came up with a bad arm.

Some people claim that we knew he had a bad arm. I didn't. He pitched like he had one when he went to the Cubs, I guess, but if his arm hurt him when he was here, I never knew it. I recently read an interview with Broglio. He said he was healthy until he hurt his arm two months after he went to the Cubs.

I like to think that I never made a deal like that, with the knowledge that someone we gave up was injured. To my knowledge, I never did.

Credit Keane

People always say I made the Brock deal, but the reason we made it was John Keane. He really liked Brock.

If I'd been sitting with Johnny Keane and asked him about Brock for Broglio and he'd said "No!" I wouldn't have made the deal. No question.

If Keane had said, "Maybe we should, and maybe we shouldn't. Let's think about it," then if I had thought about it too long, we probably wouldn't have made the deal. Remember, the trading deadline was the next day.

But Johnny Keane was an outstanding manager. He was with me in Rochester, New York, when I was general manager of our Triple A club there. I had faith in Johnny Keane. So when he said, "What are we waiting for?" I didn't wait.

Four Simple Rules

So okay, the Brock deal was a steal. But I didn't know it would be a steal. I didn't know Brock would be that good. I didn't know he would collect 3,000 hits and break all the stolen base records and go into the Hall of Fame.

When we made that trade, the Cubs were taking a chance and we were taking a chance. You win some, you lose some ... and sometimes you get lucky.

But you don't get lucky if you don't take the chance.

That leads into my four tricks for a trade:

1. You've got to need the player.
2. You've got to have good reports from your scouts and talent evaluators.
3. You've got to have the guts to make the deal.
4. You've got to get lucky.

But if you never have the guts to do anything, you'll never get lucky. You'll never give yourself the chance to be lucky.

Trader Lane

I learned how to make a deal by watching Frank Lane. I worked for him when he was general manager for the Cardinals in '56 and '57. They called him "Trader" Lane because he made a lot of deals. And he made a lot of deals he shouldn't have.

Maybe I didn't go that far, but watching him, I realized the benefit of being willing to make moves and not being too cautious—and certainly not worrying about public opinion.

Take the chance. Don't be fearful.

If you're paying attention to everybody clamoring against you—the reporters or the fans in the stands—you better get another job.

Jocketty and the Legacy

Walt Jocketty operates like that now as general manager with the Cardinals. He's taken a lot of chances and he's given himself a chance to be lucky.

And that's why he's been so successful.

Look at the players he's brought in: Jim Edmonds, Edgar Renteria, Scott Rolen, Fernando Viña, Mike Matheny, Tino Martinez, J.D. Drew.

Martinez didn't work out the way they hoped. But that list made up the whole everyday ball club last year except for Albert Pujols.

They drafted Pujols, but why is he good? Because somebody gave him a chance at age 21. Who thought Pujols would be that good at such a young age? And for his first three years? Nobody.

I know, because I've asked a lot of people in the organization. Judging talent just isn't an exact science. In most cases, it's a matter of opinion based on your evaluation and opportunity.

Some people say Pujols might be older than he claims, but who cares?

The point is that the manager, Tony La Russa, said, "Let's play him," and Walt Jocketty backed him up. They decided to put Pujols in there at a young age, whatever it was, and to give him a chance.

Signing Keith Hernandez

We took a chance on signing Keith Hernandez in '71, during my second stretch as general manager of the Cardinals.

Hernandez didn't want to sign after we drafted him out of high school. We were offering way below the money he wanted.

He was from Northern California. Bill Sayles, our scout up there, was pushing for him. He called up and said, "How come we're not signing Keith Hernandez?"

I said the kid wanted too much money. And Bill Sayles said, "I think you're missing the boat. He's playing even better since you drafted him. Why don't you send someone up to cross-check him?"

So we sent Bob Kennedy.

And Kennedy called me back right away and said, "I don't know about the money. But if you don't sign this kid, you'll regret it the rest of your life!"

As a general manager, these are the kind of answers you want:

"What are we waiting for?"

"You'll be sorry if you don't."

As a general manager, give me those kinds of people giving me those kinds of answers.

Signing Mike Shannon

Joe Monahan was the local scout here when we tried out Mike Shannon. Joe liked him and recommended him. So we had Shannon in for a workout before a game at the old Sportsman's Park in May or June of 1958. And Shannon had a good workout. A really good workout. He hit a couple of balls into the left field seats.

We were playing Cincinnati, and I happened to look behind me in the box seats back of home plate. And Gabe Paul and Birdie Tebbetts were watching batting practice. Gabe was the general manager of Cincinnati and Birdie was the manager.

I told Joe, "You better get Shannon in here and get him signed, because Gabe Paul and Birdie Tebbetts are out here. And they saw what we saw."

So we went inside and the switchboard attendant, Ada Ireland, kind of whispered to me, "Don Faurot's on the phone for you."

Don Faurot was the athletic director at the University of Missouri and a friend of mine. Shannon was a great high school football player, and he was just finishing his first year at Mizzou on a football scholarship. Freshmen weren't eligible then, but he had played in spring practice for Dan Devine—no relation to me— who was in his first year as head coach at Mizzou.

When I picked up the phone, Faurot said, "I understand you're trying to sign Mike Shannon."

I said, "That's right. He's in my office right now."

Faurot said, "He's going to be our starting quarterback next fall, and we're going to change our whole offensive system to fit his ability. Do you mind if I talk to him?"

I said fine, I didn't mind.

People might wonder why I didn't just hang up and try to sign the kid without any interference. Well, I didn't want Shannon second-guessing himself afterward if he ever found out about that call. He might resent not hearing what their plans were for him at Mizzou. And I didn't want the people at Mizzou feeling that we undercut their efforts. Hey, Mizzou football was a big thing. I didn't want that cloud over me. I just felt like they should get their shot. I know that's what I'd want if I were in their place.

So I asked Shannon if he wanted to talk to Faurot, and he said, "Yeah, I'll talk to him."

Which was typical Shannon. A lot of guys, including me, would have said, "Tell him I don't want to talk to him." I wouldn't want that pressure when I was trying to make a big decision like that.

I put Shannon on the phone in my office and closed the door and waited outside. I'm guessing it was 10 minutes before he came out.

I said, "What do you want to do?"

And he said, "I'm ready to sign with the Cardinals."

Saving Mike Shannon

In 1962, Shannon was at our Triple A club in Atlanta. One day I got a call from Harry Walker, our manager there. He said that Shannon had just quit, that he left the team and came home to St. Louis, where he grew up.

Walker told me that Shannon said, "I can't be away from my family. I've got to take care of the children and help my wife out at home."

I called Shannon and brought him into the office, and he confirmed that to me.

Then I said, "What about your career?"

He said, "Forget about it. I've got to take care of this matter first at home."

I asked him what he was going to do. And he said something like, "How the heck do I know? Maybe I'll drive a truck."

So Shannon left. I thought he was done with baseball.

Later that day, I was talking to Johnny Keane, who was our manager then, about another matter. Then I mentioned that Shannon had quit.

Keane said, "I remember him from spring training. I didn't see a lot of him, but I liked what I saw. Let's put him on the big-league club. We'll make him the 25th guy."

We had 25-man rosters then. I asked Keane if he really wanted to do that.

He said, "The 25th guy doesn't play much anyway. What difference does it make? This way, he can stay home and—who knows?—it might save his career."

I guess a lot of general managers wouldn't have gone to the manager with something like that. But I thought enough of Keane that I went to him with everything. And that started in Rochester in the early '50s, when I was the general manager and he was my manager.

We put Shannon on the big-league club, and he played 10 games for us in '62.

Two years later, he was playing in the World Series in the outfield. Three years after that, he ended up at third base and in the World Series again.

If Johnny Keane hadn't suggested making Shannon the 25th man, I'd never have thought about putting him on the club. I thought it was a heck of a gesture.

So good for Johnny. Good for the organization. And good for Mike. Because otherwise, he would have been out of baseball.

Singing Shannon's Praises

I claim that Mike Shannon's the biggest overachiever I've ever known. It's because of his work ethic.

Just look what he's done.

He came out of high school known as a football player who also played baseball. He played better in the big leagues than he did at Triple A. He was an outfielder who became a third baseman.

He became a restaurateur. He sold tickets for us before he went into the broadcast booth. And who thought he'd be the kind of broadcaster he has turned out to be?

The other guy I'd put up there is Albert Pujols. He's worked to make himself better every year. After he had that great rookie year, people said he'd drop off. He got even better. And he was better still his third year.

We like to give credit to people who achieve. Well, I think achievers are fine ... but overachievers are great.

As a general manager, those are the types you want on your ball club.

A MAN OF CHARACTER

MIKE SHANNON
REFLECTS ON BING DEVINE

Bing Devine is one of the all-time fantastic executives. He handles people so well. When I had to come home from the minors that time, in '62 I guess it was, I told Bing, "Hey, I've got some problems I have to attend to. My wife's pregnant and her doctors told her she has to stay in bed. We've got three young kids running around, and she has to stay off her feet or she's going to lose this baby. So I have to go home and take care of her."

See, we had all those kids right in a row, one a year for four years.

Bing heard that, and he said, "You go take care of what you have to take care of."

I did. After a while, Bing called to see how we were doing. I said, "Things are a lot better."

And he said, "Well, if you played here in St. Louis, do you think you could come back and play some?"

I said, "Well, let me see what happens here."

After a while my wife got better, the doctor said everything was good, so I called Bing back and said, "Yeah, I'm ready to play."

I joined the ball club, and I remember Johnny Keane put me in center field. The first guy up hit a line a drive—a smoking line drive—right at me. I caught that and I said, "Well, I guess I'm okay!"

I learned so much from Bing Devine. So many different things, so many great sayings that I can remember. He could have run General Motors, Monsanto—anything. And even at his age today, he's still sharp as a tack. You know, his mother lived to be a hundred and five years old.

I'll never forget, Bing and I were at a banquet once on the dais. I said, "Do you have a really good retirement plan?"

He looked at me kind of strange and he said, "Why would you ask me that?"

I said, "Well, just think. If your mother lived to be a hundred and five, you're going to live to be a hundred and ten or a hundred and twenty. Now I know why you were general manager of the baseball Cardinals and president of the football Cardinals. You needed two pensions!"

Man, when you think about it, who's ever been the general manager of a baseball team and the president of a football team in the same city? No one's ever done that, to my knowledge. It just shows his great ability. He's such a phenomenal manager, a phenomenal executive.

The day I signed with the Cardinals, when he put me on the phone first to talk to Don Faurot at Mizzou, that didn't surprise me.

Let me tell you something: Bing Devine is a man of character.

There was nothing back-door about this man. And all the people he hired were the same. His manager, Johnny Keane, was as honest as could be.

I went to Johnny Keane one day, I guess it was in '64, and I said, "I hit .300 on the West Coast, I think I have a chance to make the club, and my name isn't even on the board."

He said, "You know what? You're right."

So he played me for two weeks. I couldn't beg, borrow or steal a hit. I had to go back and knock on his door and say, "I've had enough. Get me out of there."

Johnny Keane said, "No, no, no. I want you in there."

I said, "Whoa, thanks a lot!"

Those are the kinds of people Bing hired.

Let me tell you something. I got sick with a serious kidney problem, you know, and had to quit playing. The doctor called Bing and said, "I think he can work as long as he's not playing ball."

So Bing called me and offered me a job.

He said, "Do you want to work?"

I said, "Yeah!"

He said, "Well, I can't pay you very much."

And I said, "I don't care, I just want to work."

So he gave me a job in the front office. I took a $2,000 pay cut to come to work. I didn't give a damn. All I wanted to do was work. They had given me up for dead six months earlier. I didn't give a damn about making money. I was tickled to death to be alive.

I went into the front office as the assistant director of promotions and sales. Bing really created a job for me, basically. Then the next year, I got a little better with my health. And he offered me two fantastic jobs. He offered me the Triple A managing job, and he offered me a coaching job in the big leagues.

I didn't think it was right, with my family situation at the time, to go off and go right back to that. So I said no. But it was really hard to get jobs then. I really felt bad about saying no.

Then Bing came to me a couple of months after that and said, "Hey, people approached me about you doing the broadcasting."

I talked to them, and it was history from there.

I think Bing probably knows me better than any other person, because we've had so much to do with one another. We've gone through a lot. And I'm telling you, he's a wonderful guy.

Hey, look at the way Bing handled that whole '64 situation, when he got fired by the Cardinals in August, and we went on and won the pennant and the World Series.

Bing Devine can handle anything. That's why the Cardinals organization was class—because of Bing Devine. Bing Devine put this organization on top. The Cardinals are class because of his class.

Chapter 2

1964:
Bittersweet Season

Branch Rickey Returns

I became general manager of the Cardinals before the 1958 season, and by the early '60s, we could see that we would soon be winning. And then Gussie Busch, who owned the team and the Anheuser-Busch brewery, brought Branch Rickey back.

As I said, I got along with Frank Lane. I can't think of anyone I didn't get along with. Even Branch Rickey.

Rickey had run the Cardinals before he left in the '40s to become general manager of the Brooklyn Dodgers. Then he ran the Pittsburgh Pirates in the '50s. He won everywhere he went. And he brought a lot of things to baseball, like spring training and the farm system and Jackie Robinson. Busch brought Rickey back right after the '62 season as a kind of senior adviser.

To be honest, I rather resented that Rickey was back. I'd been the general manager for a couple of years, and we were ready to take off. He'd been gone, he'd come back, he was in his 80s ... so let somebody else do the job.

Rickey also had Mr. Busch's ear. By design. Mr. Busch told him, "Keep me advised."

I was still the general manager in title, but he was going to run the club. Nobody told me that, but I developed that feeling. Busch gave his office at old Sportsman's Park to Rickey. Busch obviously worked mostly at the brewery, but he had this big office when he'd come to the ballpark. That office was on the first floor. Mine was a little office up on the second floor, but that was no issue. I didn't care about that.

But I sensed when Rickey came in, and we started having meetings, that he was going to be difficult if he had to deal with a strong personality. Actually, I didn't sense it. I knew it. And here's how I knew.

Rickey didn't drive a car. He had a driver, but one time the driver was unavailable. We were at the ballpark, and Rickey asked me if I'd drive him to his daughter's house in Ladue where he was staying, which was close to where I lived.

We got in my car, and Rickey was sitting in the front seat. Every time we got together, we talked baseball the whole time. So we were talking baseball, and suddenly Rickey said to me, "Why do you think I'm here?"

I said, "I think Mr. Busch wanted someone with your background and experience, being a great baseball man, to help me with the club."

Then he said, "Are we going to have trouble if I'm here to run the club?"

And I said, "Mr. Rickey, we're not *going* to have trouble. We *have* trouble right now."

My heart was pounding. It was a shock for me to hear him say what he said, and I'm sure it was a shock for him to hear me say what I said.

When I was in school, I was one of those meek little guys who never caused a problem. And when I first started working for the Cardinals out of college, as an office boy in '39, Rickey was the general manager. I didn't work for him—I was in the public relations office—but I had to run errands for Rickey. I'd get him some coffee, or I'd run out and buy him a newspaper.

Mary Murphy was his secretary then. And one day she asked me, "Is he giving you any money for the coffee and the newspaper?"

I said no.

She said, "Well, you're supposed to see me when he sends you out for something. I'll give you the money."

I was hardly making anything then, but I didn't think to ask. That's called growing up on the job. But that's how meek I was as a kid. And that's probably how Rickey remembered me. I still called him Mr. Rickey in person, because I had that respect for him.

But my conversation in the car with Rickey was post-Frank Lane. I told you how watching Lane made me more aggressive in my job. And a good example of it was when I told Rickey: "We're not *going* to have trouble. We *have* trouble right now!"

Rickey really didn't want to talk much after I said that. That kind of put a period to the conversation. I guess he wanted to think about what I said.

And I wondered, "What's this going to lead to? Am I going to get fired?"

Acquiring Dick Groat

That conversation with Rickey in my car led to a kind of truce. I was still in charge, but Rickey still had Busch's ear. And I knew that.

So I had to figure out a way to make this all work. Like when I wanted to get Dick Groat from Pittsburgh to play shortstop for us in '63.

We were giving up a young infielder named Julio Gotay. I knew we had to find a way to get an okay from Busch with Rickey now in the picture. Rickey hated giving up young players for veteran players. That's how he built the Cardinals the first time he was here, by stocking the club with young players—I knew that from my days as an office boy with the club.

So I had to set it up so that Rickey would approve the Groat deal and take it to Mr. Busch. I did this in spring training at old Al Lang Field, our ballpark in St. Petersburg, Florida.

I knew I had to get someone with me, speaking on behalf of the deal. So I got the baseball people who were closest to me, who liked Groat and who would be on my side. I think Harry "The Hat" Walker, who was managing in the minors for us, was there, and Eddie Stanky, a player personnel man, along with one or two others.

I took them to Al Lang Field during a game and surrounded myself with them. We were in Rickey's box, where I could catch him pretty easily and pack the house.

I said, "Mr. Rickey"—as I said, I always called him Mr. Rickey, for sure—"I want to talk to you about the Groat deal, which I know you know about."

I hadn't told him about it, but he always knew everything that was going on with the club.

I said, "I want to trade Gotay for Groat, and I've got other people in the deal, and I'd like your approval."

Rickey looked around and said, "You've kind of loaded this meeting for me, haven't you?"

I said, "Well, I know it looks like that, but we need Groat to make this team go."

And Rickey said, "I'm going to have a hard time adjusting myself to trading a young ballplayer for an old ballpayer, because I'm a young ballplayer man."

After a long conversation, he said, "I'll talk to the boss. I'll tell him I don't like to get rid of young prospects for veteran players. But I won't negate the deal. I'll tell him you feel strongly about it and that he should do what he wants to do."

Mr. Busch wound up okaying the deal. I think Dick Meyer, Busch's right-hand man at the brewery, probably helped.

Dick wouldn't have said, "You better do what Bing Devine wants to do." But I'm sure Dick worked around to it conveniently. He could be tough. He was in charge of almost everything Mr. Busch was involved in, but he did it in a gracious way.

Standing Up for Stan

At the start of the '63 season, Rickey thought it was time for Stan Musial to retire.

Stan wanted to play another year. Keane thought he could be a productive player. I didn't disagree—again getting back to that point that a manager's word is all-important, aside from the technical problems of contracts and salaries.

Rickey always felt—and I say this without criticism on my part—that it was time to get a younger player into the system. Stan was near the end of the line, but he wasn't there yet. So he played in '63 and hit .255 with 12 homers, splitting time in left field with Charlie James.

We finished in second place, six games back of Los Angeles, and *The Sporting News* voted me Executive of the Year.

Getting Fired

I never was looking for an open-field fight with Branch Rickey, but I liked to protect my area. That didn't mean giving up any authority. It meant trying to live comfortably with the situation, making the best of a difficult position, and not challenging by saying, "Either we do it my way or I quit." But the Groat trade early in '63 started cooling the relationship between Rickey and me.

If you look back at the middle of August in '64, the Cardinals were seven or eight games out of first place. Gussie Busch had never been associated with anything at the brewery in which he hadn't been the best. And then he bought the ball club and had been with it for over 10 years.

And he hadn't won.

Another thing that might have affected Mr. Busch was that we had a problem in the clubhouse. It involved Groat and Johnny Keane, the manager. I talked to Keane, who admitted that there had been a problem. He told me that he had handled it and not to get myself into a frenzy about it.

I really didn't remember the details until recently, when I looked through a box of old newspaper clippings. Groat was upset because Keane took away his privilege of calling the hit-and-run himself whenever he was at bat. Keane felt he was putting it on too often.

Groat had been unhappy all season. Keane talked to him once about it, but the problem wasn't resolved. So around the All-Star break in July, I told Keane to call a clubhouse meeting and confront Groat and get it resolved.

Which he did.

The reason I didn't remember all of these details is that this kind of thing went on with all clubs occasionally. You settled it in the clubhouse, and that was it. It wasn't something we needed to jump up and do something drastic about.

But then the word got back to Mr. Busch that this problem was going on.

When Dick Meyer and I used to talk, he would say about Busch, "Remember, he doesn't want to find out about something after the fact."

But I didn't think this was that big of a deal. I probably said to Keane, "Let's not bother him about it."

It was important, but it wasn't all-consuming. I was going to tell Mr. Busch about it later. In the meantime, as was so often the case, he got word about it. Even though it was all over, and I told him it was settled, the mere fact that he hadn't heard about it at the time still bothered him.

Busch was upset. I remember that. And that may have affected his thinking about me. His approach was, "If that's going on, what else is going on?"

That came back to me through Meyer, who said: "I know you handled this, but he thinks it's an example of other things that are wrong with the team."

There was kind of a fine line there with Mr. Busch. You tried to protect—not necessarily yourself—but him from all the little things. You didn't want to bother him with all the little details. But if it was something that he heard through another party, then he would wonder, "Why wasn't I told of this?"

So, often, it was a no-win situation. As time went on, you had to develop a feel for what had to be brought up and what was unimportant.

That Groat situation was an issue. But I don't think that's why Busch fired me. I really think it had more to do with us being so far back in August, which to him looked like another blown season. And Busch also had been around so long that he had many great contacts everywhere. They all had opinions, and he would listen to many different people.

So he decided to fire me. And nothing that Dick Meyer or Al Fleishman or anyone else said on my behalf was going to change it.

Al liked me. I knew that. He handled public relations for Mr. Busch, who leaned on him a lot. But Al didn't have any control. And I knew Dick liked me. He was the one who put himself on the line to hire me after I was general manager of our Triple A team in Rochester, New York.

But Busch's mind was made up.

One day, Al called me and said, "You have a meeting with Mr. Busch."

I said, "Is that tomorrow?"

Al said, "Yes. You know what's going to happen?"

I said, "No, what?"

He said, "You're going to get fired."

I was shocked and angry. Yeah, I had recognized that I was fighting a battle. But I wasn't just fighting to build a club. I was fighting for my position and my prestige.

It might sound like Al was being a little harsh with me, but he really did me a favor. When I went down to see Busch at the brewery the next day, August 17, 1964, I was ready for it. It wasn't that I went in there thinking I could make a case for myself. I knew the case was done. And that was better than going in there with high hopes.

When Al had told me I'd be fired the next day, he said, "Whatever you do, don't burn any bridges."

I'd like to think I wouldn't have burned bridges anyway, but it didn't hurt to have an expert's advice. And if there were two guys whom I listened to, they were Al Fleishman and Dick Meyer.

Technically, I resigned. They wanted me to resign because it saved them the face of firing me. It was easier to say, "Bing Devine resigned."

I didn't object to that. It seemed like the thing to do at the time. From my standpoint, I was a Cardinals man all my life, as a kid and a fan before I was an employee. If that's what they wanted me to do, then that's what I'd do. And through the media contacts with Al Fleishman, he made sure they knew I was really fired anyway.

When it was all over, I went to New York for three years, with the Mets. Then I came back to the Cardinals as general manager again.

And when I came back, Al Fleishman told me, "You made the proper approach when you left here in '64. You didn't make a battle out of this. You didn't fight it. You didn't say anything bad about anybody.

"Even though you didn't know you'd ever be back, you handled yourself properly. And that's why Mr. Busch brought you back."

Al used to tell people that I was the only person Gussie Busch ever hired twice ... and fired twice.

Because Mr. Busch eventually fired me again.

A Keane Friend

As I said, there's no question in my mind that I got fired because Mr. Busch was frustrated. He'd always had success with Anheuser-Busch. He'd owned the Cardinals for 10 years, give or take, and he was tired of not succeeding in this other business.

So he decided to make a change in August when we were eight or 10 games out of first place.

To my knowledge, Mr. Busch never issued any directive that Keane was to be fired too. But there were rumors—and I think they may have been well founded—that Keane was a lame duck after I was gone and that Mr. Busch was considering a new manager.

After I got fired, the team started playing well, and the Phillies fell apart. The Cardinals won the pennant and the World Series under Johnny Keane. And then he quit and went to New York to manage the Yankees.

The background to this was 1-2-3, as I see it.

1. Keane and I were very close.

2. He regretted, if not resented, that I got fired in August.

3. Keane knew the rumors that he was a lame duck. I think it hurt his pride. And then, just because he won the pennant and the World Series, everything was supposed to be fine?

I think he resented that.

The story I heard was that the brewery had decided to make a long-term deal with Keane after the World Series. So they set up a press conference to announce Keane's extension, but he rejected it and went to the Yankees.

Keane never told me what he was doing. He never even mentioned it to Lela, his wife. If he had told me that he was quitting, I'd like to think I would have talked him out of it, because he was the right personality for St. Louis. He grew up here. He was not the right fit for New York, and he took over a club that was old and about to go downhill. The Yankees were aging and deteriorating.

It was just an unfortunate time to move to New York. And it didn't last long. He was gone, 20 games into his second year in '66, and he died that off season after he was fired.

We were so close from the years at Rochester together and after I brought him to St. Louis to manage. I didn't think he needed to—or should have—quit the Cardinals because of me.

But Johnny Keane was a loyal guy, and that's how he felt.

Rickey "Resigns"

When I was fired in '64, Branch Rickey was pretty sharp. He wasn't the kind of guy to challenge things openly.

He knew he wasn't going to be the general manager at his age—he was almost 83—so he recommended Bob Howsam. Dick Meyer saw that Howsam was very close to Rickey and that Rickey would really run the club, maybe under the table. Dick didn't like that.

So after the season, Dick said to Mr. Busch, "You've got your own man in there now in Howsam. I think we ought to get Rickey out of the picture. He's served his purpose."

That was Dick's way of feeling better about what happened to me. I know, because Dick later told me what he did.

Officially, Rickey also resigned three days after Keane quit. But what happened was that Dick called Howsam into his office down at Anheuser-Busch and told him, "We've got to get rid of Rickey, and you're going to fire him."

Howsam said, "I'll see him down at the Instructional League in St. Petersburg, and I'll tell him then."

Dick said, "No, we're not going to do it that way. You know where he is. You pick up the telephone right now and call him and tell him. It's going to happen right now. We're not putting this thing off."

So Howsam did it. It was tough for him. I know how he felt. Rickey had brought him in as general manager, just like Dick Meyer had brought me in. And Howsam wanted some time to figure out how to tell him.

But Dick had a purpose. He resented that Rickey was put in there above me in the first place and that I was put in that kind of position. And he had the feeling that I'd been submarined, that Rickey undermined me. But in fairness to Rickey, he undermined me because Busch really wanted him to.

I knew that Busch was just frustrated that we hadn't won, but I knew we were close when I got fired in August of '64. Then we had the sensational finish, the Phillies fell apart, and we won the pennant and the World Series.

It was the same team that was there when I left. They didn't make any moves after I was gone. I had traded for guys like Bill White, Julian Javier, Curt Flood, and Groat. I kept Frank Lane from trading Ken Boyer. Tim McCarver came up through our system. So did Mike Shannon.

That I was sitting on the sidelines watching the World Series was a happy coincidence and a bittersweet thing.

Executive of the Years

The *Sporting News* named me baseball Executive of the Year for '64, which was nice because it was a vote by the other general managers. They had honored me the year before, too, when we finished second.

But I didn't gloat when I got the award again after being fired. I don't think that's my nature.

Well, maybe gloating was in me to begin with. But as you go through these things in life, you realize you've got to take care of the business ahead of you. Feeling sorry for yourself, being angry, being bitter—there's no benefit to it. Period. That's the luck of the draw, and you move on.

They had a dinner for me in St. Louis after the '64 season. I got up and said, "This is a hard way to gain some fame. There's a lot of regret, but no resentment. And you feel a lot of emotion. If you weren't a grown man, you'd cry."

At the dinner, someone read a telegram from Buzzie Bavasi, the general manager of the Los Angeles Dodgers. It was addressed to:

"The only man fired in between two Executive of the Year awards."

I guess that's an honor that I still hold. But for the sake of every other GM out there, I hope that's one record of mine that will never be broken!

HANDLING HIS SETBACKS LIKE A SAINT

BOB BROEG REFLECTS ON BING DEVINE

D er Bingle, as I called him, and I started with the Cardinals on the same day in 1939. He was full-time, making 65 dollars per month. I was part-time for the summer, making 20 dollars a week.

After I went to the *Post-Dispatch* and covered the team and became sports editor, I always kidded him about that, that I got paid more part-time than he did full-time.

I've known him all these years, and he's a saint. He's Prince Valiant, Sir Galahad. He had to be, the way he handled what happened to him in '64.

I grew up in St. Louis, and I'd waited 18 years for a pennant. When Tim McCarver caught the pennant-winning pop foul, it was a moment of great joy. But it was bittersweet to me because of what happened to Bing.

It was a travesty. And a lot of the players on the team felt the same way.

Bob Howsam did nothing to win the pennant after he became GM. He led the league in cheers. Rickey had been close to him because Howsam had lost some money in Denver in the Continental League, which Rickey was involved in before coming back to St. Louis.

If they hadn't won, Keane would have been gone after the season. Keane knew the handwriting was on the outfield wall. He was in daily communication with Devine during the season, but Howsam ignored him.

When Leo Durocher was coaching for the Dodgers, Harry Caray, who was still broadcasting Cardinals games, took him down to see Gussie. The rumor got out that Durocher was hired in secret to replace Keane after the season.

Everyone denied it. Maybe it wasn't supposed to be true, but it was. Durocher had resigned from the Dodgers late in the season, and he told the press he quit because he had a big-league manager's job waiting for him next year.

The Cardinals had finished the first half of the season at 40-41. After the All-Star Game, I went to the Cardinals players and asked them off the record, without identification, what they needed.

Everybody answered "relief pitching." Except Bob Gibson. He wouldn't answer. And Bill White said, "I won't answer unless you use my name." Then he said, "I'm the reason. Look at how I'm hitting. I'm not driving in any runs."

It turned out that the solution was achieved in a clubhouse meeting I didn't know about, which was held at just about the same time.

Dick Groat had been relieved of his automatic hit-and-run privilege early in the year by Keane. He finally took it away from Groat one day when McCarver was on first. Groat kept putting on the hit and run, and he kept fouling off pitches. McCarver kept running every time till he was worn out.

Dick was a great guy, but he was a flannel mouth. He flapped his mouth. He talked too much. And he boo-hooed a lot. He boo-hooed about Keane to Eddie Mathews, the Braves' third baseman, who was dating Gussie Busch's daughter.

In the meantime, Bing had heard about it. He told Keane to call a clubhouse meeting and clear it up. So Keane called the meeting and confronted Groat, and Groat admitted it and apologized in front of the team. And he shut up his mouth after that. This was right around the All-Star break in July.

When Bing saw Gussie after that, he didn't say anything because he didn't think it was a problem. But Gussie thought it was. His daughter had told him about trouble in the clubhouse.

Gussie said to Bing, "Are you sure you don't have anything to tell me?"

Bing innocently disavowed it. Gussie didn't like that.

The club started climbing after the All-Star break. They called in Shannon from Atlanta, the Triple A team, to play right field. He had a strong arm.

I told Jim Toomey, the club's PR man, "This is the best line-up you've had all year."

Devine's team was winning. They were seven or eight games out in the middle of August, but they were eight or nine games over .500 after being 40-41 at the halfway point.

In other words, they were already en route.

But when Rickey returned to the Cardinals, he regarded Bing as his glorified office boy, which is what Bing was when he started in '39. Rickey was an impediment. He was undercutting Bing. We all knew that. I even did a Cardinal Richelieu column about Rickey.

While all this was going on, Busch also had gotten ticked off at the club's little business manager, Art Routzong. He rubbed Gussie the wrong way, and Gussie told Bing to fire him.

Bing said, "I don't want to do it."

Routzong ended up being fired anyway, and Gussie said to Bing, "You go, too."

I was shocked, like Bing and everyone else. I never saw that coming.

When the Cardinals went on and won the pennant and the World Series, Rickey took a lot of heat. Then Keane quit and went to the Yankees, which was another shocker. I was so sure that Keane would sign a new contract that I flew to cover a Notre Dame football game.

The next day, I would say this was the most dramatic front page in my history at the *Post-Dispatch*: Khruschev was fired. Red Russia showed they had the atomic bomb. Yogi Berra was fired as manager of the Yankees. And Johnny Keane quit as manager of the Cardinals.

Then I broke a story about a memo Rickey wrote that August, right before Bing was fired.

I got this mysterious assistance from a gal who worked in the front office. I didn't want to use it, because they'd know who gave it to me and they might fire her. But she said she was quitting to join the Houston club.

So I used the memo. Rickey said in it that, "If by such and such a date we're so far out of the race, here's what I would do …"

He wanted to send Shannon and Dal Maxvill and Barney Schultz to the minors and bring up some kids like Nelson Briles for a look. In other words, Rickey was writing off the season.

But all three of those guys—Shannon, Maxie and Schultz—were key guys down the stretch. Schultz led the team in saves, the relief pitching that the players all said they needed back at the All-Star break.

Rickey tried to say that was just writing a note to himself, but why put it in a memo? He lost a lot of credibility when I wrote about that memo. He was already taking a lot of heat because Bing's team won and because Keane quit after finding out that Rickey had secretly hired Durocher to replace him.

One other thing happened after that season. Groat wrote a bread-and-butter letter to members of the press, thanking the writers for their coverage.

I wrote back and said, "That's nice, Dick, and I'm glad you won, but unfortunately you were the direct cause of Bing getting fired."

Then in spring training, we talked about it face to face. Groat said he was sorry as hell about Bing being left out.

I said, "So am I. But it's too late now."

Chapter 3

Creating the
Miracle Mets

Keeping Jerry Koosman

After I got fired by the Cardinals, I went to the New York Mets in September of '64. I stayed until the end of the '67 season.

I was brought in for a top-level administrative job, kind of waiting in the wings for George Weiss to retire as president and general manager. My original title with the Mets was special assistant to the president.

The guy I was closest to there was Joe McDonald, who went on to become general manager with the Cardinals when Whitey Herzog was manager in the '80s. Joe and I got in cahoots to manipulate George Weiss and get things done.

George had a lot of success with the Yankees in the '50s and early '60s, and he was looked upon as the premier general manager of that time. Now he was getting ready to retire, and I was supposed to replace him. But he wasn't going to let some young guy come in and run the office while he was still there.

At one point George said, "We're going to get rid of Jerry Koosman."

Koosman was a young left-handed pitcher in the minors, but he didn't make that much of an impression on George's guys running the farm system. Joe McDonald and I thought it was a mistake to give up on Koosman. Then we found out that George really hated to get rid of players who owed the club money. It wasn't unusual then for players to borrow small amounts to live on, because they made so little money in the minors. The home office would just deduct some of the money due from every paycheck till the player paid it all back.

In fact, when I was the business manager in Johnson City in Class D ball, I borrowed money from my future wife, Mary, so I could eat breakfast. I never did pay her back. I'm surprised she didn't dump me. And if you talk to her, she'll say, "I'm surprised I didn't, too!"

Koosman only owed the Mets something like $500. But George wanted that money back.

Joe McDonald said, "I'll keep putting it out to George that Koosman still owes us money and that we better keep him till we get all of it back."

So that's what Joe did. George never did trade Koosman, and he ended up winning 17 games for the Mets in '69 and two more when they won the World Series against Baltimore.

Drawing Tom Seaver

Joe McDonald and I had to backdoor other things when George Weiss was the Mets' GM. That's how we got Tom Seaver.

Seaver had been pitching at Southern California and was a top-level prospect in '66. This was before we had the draft, and he'd already been signed by Atlanta. But one of the rules then was that you couldn't sign a college player before he played his last game. The Braves signed Seaver before Southern Cal played a Marine Corps base team. There was some question whether a Marine Corps team counted as a real game on the schedule. But the commissioner, William Eckert, held a hearing, and Seaver was declared a free agent.

The ruling was that his contract was valid, but that they'd have a drawing for any other club to enter except the Braves. The team that won the drawing would have to pay the contract, which was for $40,000.

Joe McDonald and I had trouble convincing George Weiss that we should go into the drawing. George said, "We don't have proof that he's worth that kind of money."

Remember, $40,000 back then was like $4 million now.

But I thought: If you're losing 100 games a year and competing for attention in New York with the Yankees, you'd better do something. So Joe McDonald and I talked George into it a day or two before the drawing.

We theorized that George finally gave in because we had been talking about Seaver using so many facts and figures. George probably thought: "If he's that good, then 12 or 15 teams will be in the pool ... and our chance will be slim of getting him anyway."

But George didn't know that our chances were one in three! The only three clubs in the pool were the Mets, Philadelphia and Cleveland.

I can remember getting the call from Lee MacPhail, who was an executive in the commissioner's office. I took the call, and he told me, "You've got Seaver."

Forty years later, the whole thing is indelible in my mind.

I remember thinking, "Great!"

And then, "Uh-oh, Joe and I are in trouble!"

But when we told George, he just shrugged his shoulders, as if to say, "So be it."

Even though we were paying Seaver a lot of money, we actually gave him a little bonus when we won his rights. We liked him, and we wanted him happy because he wasn't going to the team of his choice.

And he was worth it.

Tom Seaver was Rookie of the Year in '67. He won 25 games when the Mets won the World Series in '69. He won his first Cy Young Award that year, and then he won two more, all with the Mets. He wound up with 311 wins in the big leagues and is in the Hall of Fame.

I didn't know all of that would happen when Joe McDonald and I convinced George Weiss to go after him. I hadn't even seen Seaver pitch before that drawing, but our scouts liked him. And I'd learned from Frank Lane that if you don't do anything, you'll never do anything wrong ... but you'll never do anything right, either.

No Ordinary Joe

Joe McDonald had started in the Mets' organization with some office job, and by the time I got there in '64 he was a low-level guy in the minor league department. When I left in '67, he was really my right-hand man, the assistant to the president and general manager, which was my title.

He had a great work ethic. It always comes back to work ethic with people I admire, and I admired Joe.

When I first got to New York, he was a great contact for me. He was one of those guys who knew where the bodies were buried. He'd tip me off on certain people—and certain directions to go or not to go.

He was very trustworthy. He was willing to take a stand, which as I said was very important to me. He'd give you an opinion and he wouldn't back down, no matter what you thought about it. And he was very perceptive. He was right about Koosman and he was right about Seaver. It's one thing to have an opinion and stick to it, but that's not much good if your opinion is misguided.

So it didn't surprise me when Joe went on to become Whitey Herzog's right-hand man when the Cardinals won the World Series in '82.

Help in the Big Apple

When I got to New York, I was a complete stranger. Not only to the Mets, but to the city. Guys like Harold Weissman and Jim Thomson were with the club then, and I leaned on them.

Weissman was the PR man. Thomson was like the sergeant-at-arms for the Mets. He knew where all the bodies were buried or were going to be buried. I not only listened to them, but I made sure to ask questions if I didn't know something. They kept me out of a lot of trouble when I was in New York.

New York Media

I guess the New York writers kind of grew on me. If you're going to waste your time on—or become too tied up in—what the media people say, for or against you, then you've got a problem.

I was never unavailable, that's for sure. I learned that from Frank Lane when I worked for him with the Cardinals. If he made a deal, he liked to talk about it whether it was big or little, a good deal or a bad deal. He wanted to have his name attached to it.

And you know what? It dawned on me that these writers have a job to do, and their bosses are obviously satisfied with them because they've still got a job. So when they have an opinion or a commentary that you don't like or don't think is fair, you just shake it off.

Many people were intimidated by Dick Young, the columnist for the New York *Daily News*. I was a little bit careful or cautious around him and a couple others who could be pretty rough. But that's their right and that's their job.

Dick Young was the first guy whom I had in mind when I said to myself about the New York writers, "They're not going to get fired because I don't like what they say about me, so I better get along with them."

Sure, I had my favorites through the years, like Bob Broeg. We'd been friends since 1939 when we were both office boys with the Cardinals. But I always tried to get along with the guys who weren't so friendly. You've got your job to do and they've got theirs. And you shouldn't let the other's job affect your own.

I managed to put up pretty well with both acclaim and criticism from the New York writers. I think they recognized that I did an adequate job.

Casey and Whitey

When I got to the Mets, Casey Stengel was still managing them. I liked him. If you couldn't get along with Casey Stengel, you couldn't get along with anybody. And there's no way you could be around him and not learn from him.

Mostly what I learned was to take a more personal approach to life. He made you realize that baseball is big, and baseball is great, and baseball is your business . . . but have some fun. Life is a lot of things, and humor is part of it.

It hurt him to lose. If you look at his history with the Yankees, you know that. He was used to going to the World Series every year, and the Mets were losing 100 games or more every year.

It was the same story every day with the Mets. So when the writers came around, Casey would talk and come up with something new that they could write a story about.

In the middle of the '65 season, Casey broke his hip in a fall at a restaurant. He had to retire, and we promoted Wes Westrum to replace him.

The next year, we hired a young coach from the Oakland Athletics named Whitey Herzog to coach third base. I never really knew Whitey before that, even though we were both from St. Louis. New York is where I really got to know him.

If you think about it, Whitey became a little like Casey. When Casey was there, he was the great contact for the media. And when

Whitey came in to coach, he became the great contact for the media. He'd give the writers a line when they came to him, and he started filling that in just like Casey did. Whitey was funny and he was easy to understand. I always said that Casey didn't make quick sense. But after you finished mulling what he said over in your mind, it did make sense.

One time, we were scheduled to play a night game in Los Angeles, and there was a prospect out there whom everybody liked—a catcher. He was a good hitter, a left-handed bat and a good catcher, too.

The kid was playing a doubleheader in the afternoon, so I thought it would be great to bring Casey up to see this prospect who everyone thought was so great. The kid got up like eight times in the doubleheader and only made a couple of outs. So we were driving back for our Mets ballgame, and I asked Casey, "What do you think about that kid?"

And Casey said, "Six or seven hits out of eight? What else do I need to say?"

I thought that made perfect sense. But as it turned out, the kid got a bad back after a couple of years and never fulfilled expectations.

Whitey Moves Up

Whitey Herzog was 34 years old when we made him our player development director with the Mets.

I didn't think that was so young. As a player and a coach, he was on the front line. He was a third base coach at 33. I didn't think of it at the time, but that was pretty young for *that* job.

But seeing Whitey in the dugout and the clubhouse, all you had to do was ask him a question and he'd start talking. It was interesting to hear him talk. It still is! I just ran into him the other day, and he hasn't changed. Whitey was the kind of guy who'd give you an answer on anything. Right or wrong, he's going to give you an opinion. And he wouldn't change his mind if somebody challenged him.

I just thought he had something more to offer than he did as a player and then as a coach. He used to impress me as having all the qualifications to be a top-level executive. And later he became a top manager and general manager in the big leagues.

What I liked about Whitey back then was his overall knowledge of player personnel. Not only our players with the Mets, but across the major leagues. And I knew he'd be getting to know the minor leagues, too.

As a player development director, you have to have an eye for a prospect's ability. You also have to have a good staff of managers and coaches in the minors, and a good relationship with them. We had a pretty good organization in place, so Whitey didn't have to worry about that. He was in a position to recommend players as prospects, the timing as far as bringing them up to the big leagues, and whether we should be putting them in any deals we were considering.

Again, I liked Whitey's willingness to take chances and make decisions. He could do that well … which was evident later, too, when he was managing.

When we promoted him to personnel director, I don't recall that I had any argument from my staff. Joe McDonald was my right-hand man. He was pretty important in terms of player development, scouting and overall knowledge of the baseball side of the organization. He knew Herzog and liked him, and liked him as a baseball man, too. That's why it didn't surprise me when they worked so well together years later in St. Louis.

Fitting In

When I came to the Mets in September of '64, I had a loose job description because George Weiss hadn't left yet as general manager. I didn't officially become president and general manager until November of '67. That's what the history books say. And that's technically correct. But I was really acting as the general manager all along.

It's not an easy relationship to describe. George and I were joint GMs, or whatever you want to call it. We were partnering. Again, the relationship was such that he knew I was there to succeed him. In that sense, it was like Rickey-Devine, except in this case I was a younger man coming in to take over for an older man, instead of the other way around with Branch Rickey and me.

What ownership had really told me in New York was, "You're in a position to take over, but we're not going to force this thing on George Weiss. But if you see something that you don't think is right, a deal that is being made or not being made, come to us and we'll do it."

Well, I didn't want to do that. And I didn't. That's what had happened to me with Rickey while I was with the Cardinals.

I know that most people are bound to come in and take charge in a situation like that. And I did bring my secretary from St. Louis, Marilyn Schroeder, with me. But I dislike confrontations with people I'm working with or for. I try to solve most problems satisfactorily when they tie in with personnel. I did not want to get with ownership behind George's back on any matter.

And when working with men like Rickey and George Weiss, with their background in the game, I wasn't going to say anything to denigrate them. At the same time, I didn't want them telling me what I could or couldn't do.

No matter who was kidding whom, you had to make the club better. That was too important. That came first, ahead of who had what title or whose feelings were hurt. George and I may have had two different philosophies on how to get it done. But from that standpoint, trying to make the club better, we were in the same court. And George wanted to compete with the Yankees, too. He had so much success with the Yankees for all those years, and they had let him go, just like they let Casey go.

Probably very few people knew what the arrangement was between George and me. For me to sit down and have conversations with a reporter then like we're doing now, it would have been at least unpleasant. The only one who had a close enough relationship to me to know what we were doing, and how we were trying to do it, was Joe McDonald.

I didn't want to have any secrets from George. I didn't spring anything on him. In that way, I treated him like I did Mr. Busch when I was in St. Louis. I was being careful and cautious with George. I'd say, "George, I think we can make this move," or "We think we should do that."

That's why Joe and I worked through him on things like keeping Koosman and getting Seaver. As I said, I didn't want to run to ownership as soon as George disagreed with me on something.

Most of the time when I went in to make a deal or move players through the minor leagues, George was pretty agreeable to anything we did. I don't recall him ever taking a stand against any deal we wanted to make, or that we should make, or that we did make. He was like Mr. Busch. He just wanted to know about it before we did it.

And George wasn't aggressive in those days on any deal of his own that he wanted to do. He'd come to me with it first. So it all worked out all right.

Double-Checking

So instead of just taking over when I got to New York, I thought one of the best things I could do was to get out of George's way and serve a purpose at the same time.

And he didn't disagree.

The first thing I did with the Mets in '65 was make up my mind to continue seeing the club as much as possible, and also the minor league teams. I did not let myself get away from that side of the game—player development. I thought it would be helpful for me to get a long-range picture of the organization. I wanted to get to know the scouts and their areas of the country that they covered. One way to do that was to get a look at the players they were recommending before they were drafted and signed.

Now, every organization does that and refers to it as cross-checking. It was done then, but not widely. I called it double-checking.

I thought it was best to see the prospects firsthand that our scouts were recommending for the first round of the amateur draft. In those days, the Mets always had a high draft choice because they always finished last.

Each scout in the organization had his own pick in his geographic area for that number one choice. But the scouts don't see the players in anyone else's area. So it was helpful to have somebody see as many players as possible and throw them into one pot.

I realized it would probably be more comfortable for Weiss to stay in his office in New York while I ran all over the country, double-checking on these amateur free agents. And it made sense to do it, from a baseball standpoint.

I was gone double-checking for two or three months. I'd fly in and the scout would pick me up at the airport and then we'd go to a game. We'd watch the player the scout liked, then he'd drive me back to the hotel and I'd fly out the next day for somewhere else. Very seldom did I stay more than one day to watch a player.

One of the players I saw then was Nolan Ryan.

The Ryan Express

I have to tell you that Nolan Ryan, in the game I saw, was less than impressive as a prospect.

The game was in Alvin, Texas. It was a hot day. The competition he faced was not good. And Nolan had a bad day. Let's say he didn't make much of an impression. The other club drew bases on balls and got hits off him.

Our scout there was Red Murff. He was an ex-pitcher and an experienced scout. I recall that when we were leaving after that game, Murff was almost in tears, because he had great feeling for "his" players, the ones that he recommended.

He was saying to me, "Here you are, coming in to see Ryan on a day like this, and he has a game like that. Now what'll happen?"

I said, "I'll tell you what'll happen. You've been scouting a lot longer than I have. You go ahead and put in the strongest report you want on Nolan Ryan. I obviously can't confirm it from what I saw myself, but I won't negate it. I'll just say, 'It was one game and he just had a bad day.'"

That's what we did.

But the rest of the story, as they say, is this: We didn't take Ryan in the first round. We didn't draft him till our 12th pick. But the Mets still got him.

If I wanted to, I could have killed that. Well, I'm not saying they would have said, "Oh, Bing Devine said no, so that's what we'll do." But it wouldn't have helped the situation.

So the Mets had Ryan when they won the world championship in '69. The funny thing is, four years after the World Series, they traded Ryan and three others for Jim Fregosi.

And Ryan was on his way to the Hall of Fame.

Catching Jerry Grote

I did one of my first important deals for the Mets on October 19, 1965. We got Jerry Grote from Houston for a pitcher named Tom Parsons and cash.

That was a really big thing, getting Grote. He was still young, having just turned 23, but he had established himself. We had many young pitchers, and Grote was not just a catcher. He was a Mike Matheny type. He combined great defensive ability with a knack for handling pitchers, especially young pitchers.

Grote had an outstanding capability for blocking the ball. Pitchers weren't afraid to throw to him a breaking ball down low in certain situations, which is important for a young pitcher's confidence.

And just like Matheny with the Cardinals now, Grote was not an easy out. He was not a great hitter, but he could hit in clutch situations.

After Grote came over to New York, he was even better than our expectations, handling pitchers and being a presence on the club.

The day after we acquired Grote, we traded to get Ken Boyer from the Cardinals in exchange for another third baseman named Charley Smith and a pitcher named Al Jackson.

When you think about it, the first thing I did as general manager of the Cardinals was to keep Boyer in St. Louis after Frank Lane wanted to trade him. And then one of the first things I did as general manager of the Mets was to get Boyer out of St. Louis. I had Boyer from the beginning of his career. The first club he reported to with the Cardinals was Rochester in Triple A, when I was general manager. I remembered him there. Somehow I just seem to have a natural tie to Ken Boyer.

He led the Mets in runs batted in his first year there, with 61. He was kind of a bridge. You wanted to get a little more respectable while you went along. We were waiting for the kids to develop, or to do a major deal.

Getting Tommie Agee

The Mets really got going in '67. George Weiss was totally out of the picture and we made 54 deals that season, a big-league record. We used 27 pitchers that season, which tied the big-league record.

One of our best trades that year was when we dealt an infielder named Bob Johnson, whom I don't remember, for Art Shamsky from Cincinnati.

And the last deal I made that winter of '67, before I left New York, was really a big deal for the club. I'd come to an agreement on it in December, right before I left. It was for Tommie Agee, a center fielder, and an infielder named Al Weis.

We gave up Tommy Davis, the former batting champ with the Dodgers; a pitcher named Jack Fisher; a catcher named Dick Booke; and minor-leaguer Billy Wynne.

John Murphy had been named to replace me as general manager, and I told him the deal was in place if he wanted to make it. It was just like when Frank Lane separated from the Cardinals and left me the Boyer trade if I wanted to do it.

John Murphy and I had come to know each other pretty well. And he went ahead with the Agee deal—I guess because he thought it was a pretty good deal,which it turned out to be. Agee starred in the '69 World Series against Baltimore, and Weis homered to help clinch the final game.

Let's Make a Deal

I don't think I made any deals with the Mets that I regret. How could I? We were so bad that we weren't ever going to give up much because nobody wanted our players.

And if you did make a deal that was bad, well, you were losing a hundred games anyway. So you make a deal and lose a hundred again? So what?

After I came over from St. Louis in '64, another of my first deals was with the Cardinals. We traded Tracy Stallard, the pitcher who gave up Roger Maris's 61st home run, and infielder Julio Chacon for Johnny Lewis, a left-handed-hitting outfielder, and pitcher Gordie Richardson.

When I officially took over for George, a lot of the deals we made were for cash. We had money to spend, so we might as well spend it and try to get better—obviously, with the approval of ownership.

Most likely, we didn't have anybody the other teams thought was desirable enough to want in return.

We got Frank Lary, a pitcher, for cash…Chuck Hiller, a second baseman, for cash…Dave Eilers, a pitcher, for cash…Jack Hamilton, a pitcher, for cash…Al Luplow, an outfielder, for cash…Jerry Arrigo, Bob Shaw, Bob Friend, Ralph Terry—all pitchers—for cash.

You'll notice that a lot of them were pitchers. Well, you couldn't do just one or two of those deals and hope to get better. You had to make a lot and hope for the best, hope you get lucky.

Hiring Gil Hodges

My first year with the Mets, Wes Westrum took over for Casey Stengel during the season after Casey fell and broke his hip. Westrum managed for two more years, but for long range, we needed to go in a different direction. The Mets were drawing, but they were losing a hundred games every year. They were pitied. That's why I was brought in. I said, "We've got to start getting better."

Talent was at a low level. That's why we had to make some changes all around. That's why getting Tom Seaver made great sense, even though his contract was expensive.

A lot of what they were trying to do was gain some standing on the Yankees. And our ownership wanted to get a manager of stature in there, especially someone with popularity in the New York area.

They said, "What about Gil Hodges?"

He was still managing the Washington Senators, but our ownership liked him—people like Donald Grant and Herb Walker and, as a result, Mrs. Joan Payson, the primary owner. They kind of had a fond spot for Gil Hodges.

I thought it was a good idea. Hodges had all the credentials in the world, including local stardom. He had played first base for the Brooklyn Dodgers. And he had played with the Mets in their first two years. That's when the ownership got to know him.

I don't think I really had anybody to sell as a manager who made sense from every standpoint like Hodges. So during the '67 World Series, I reached an agreement verbally with Hodges to manage the club.

The Cardinals were playing the Red Sox. I drove to the ballgame at Busch Stadium and met him there. I remember sitting down in the boxes, watching my old team play in the World Series, talking to Hodges and agreeing to a handshake deal.

After the game I drove him to the airport, and we agreed on a deal in my car on our way to Lambert Field. He flew back home and I flew to Boston. Then we had agreed to meet in Boston to finalize the deal, and he was at the press conference.

When the teams went to Boston to continue the Series, we announced Hodges's signing at a hotel there. There was some controversy then, because we broke the commissioner's recommendation not to make any major announcements that would upstage the World Series.

It might have looked that way when we announced the Hodges signing, but that's not what we were doing. I was always one for getting announcements made as quickly as possible. That way, you don't have the leaks. If more than one person knows something, you've got a problem, not a secret.

This was a big deal, so we knew it would leak. And we wanted to make a big publicity splash. Remember, we were competing with the Yankees for attention in New York.

To get the right to sign Hodges, we had to make a trade with George Selkirk, the Senators' general manager. The deal was $100,000 and a pitcher named Bill Denehy for Hodges. Denehy was a middle-ground pitcher, and he was still a prospect. But when you're that close to becoming a winner and you need a manager, you have to close the deal.

I never really knew Hodges before that. John Murphy, my assistant, had a hand in getting that deal done with the Senators. He knew Selkirk personally from the years they spent playing together with the Yankees. But since I was the general manager, I was the one who sat down with Hodges at the World Series and talked to him. And just meeting him and negotiating and signing him, he made a good impression on me. He left me with a good feeling.

But I wasn't around the next spring to watch him manage.

The Cards Come Calling

Stan Musial had been the general manager of the Cardinals in '67, and they won the pennant and the World Series.

Musial was kind of a dark horse. Nobody ever thought he'd end up as general manager. Like I always said about Stan, he never made any bad decisions. He had a great career, and then he won the World Series in one year as general manager.

In a nutshell, why stick around?

It was a perfect time to get out. And he probably found out how time-consuming the job was.

From 1964 to 1967, the Cardinals had three general managers: Bing Devine, Bob Howsam and Stan Musial. So the Cardinals were looking for a general manager to replace Musial. Dick Meyer, Gussie Busch's right-hand man at Anheuser-Busch, was in charge.

It seemed like Dick Meyer's name always came into the picture for me at important times in my career. Dick and I had been close when he made me the general manager the first time, and we had remained close. I had great admiration for him as an executive and as a man.

He knew I left my family here in St. Louis and commuted when I took the Mets job. For three years, Mary and I didn't move to New York. In the summer when our three daughters weren't in school, the family would come east and we lived up in Connecticut. Otherwise, it was a constant commute.

I say constant, but during the season I wasn't just sitting in New York. You're out on the road with the club or out seeing the minor league clubs play. I'd done that with the Cardinals, and I'd have done that no matter where we lived.

But in the off season, the girls were in school and I did have to commute from New York to see them. Sometimes I'd come home a couple of times a week, as I was traveling back and forth. I'd come in overnight for what Mary thought was an important PTA meeting, something like that to keep a connection with the kids' schools, or just to have dinner with my wife.

It wasn't easy. But remember, Shea Stadium—where our office was—is about 90 seconds from LaGuardia Airport. Somebody from the office would drive me over, and I'd just take a bag on the plane and be in the air. Same thing coming back. When I got to LaGuardia, somebody would zip over from Shea to pick me up.

Occasionally, I'd be in the office the next day before people could drive in from Long Island, depending on the traffic.

It wasn't in my contract, but the New York club did pay for those trips most of the time. Our ownership was always first-class.

Dick Meyer indicated that he talked to Mr. Busch and said, "Bing Devine left his family in St. Louis when he went to New York. His heart has always been with the Cardinals, even as a young man. Why don't we get him back?"

As Dick told me, Mr. Busch said, "Yeah, that makes sense."

And so Dick approached me and I said yes.

The Walker Rumor

Some New York reporters surmised that I left the Mets because I wanted to hire Harry Walker instead of Hodges and that ownership wouldn't let me.

It made sense. Why else would I leave? That's gotta be the way it was, right?

The only thing is that it's not true.

Did I think highly of Harry Walker? Yes. People who knew him in World War II told me he was a wild man fighting in Europe. That was hard to imagine, because he was such a friendly guy.

He managed for me twice in the minors with the Cardinals, at Rochester and at Atlanta. I thought he'd make a good manager in the major leagues, which he later proved at Pittsburgh.

But I wasn't pushing him as manager of the Mets. I left for the reasons I said all along. I missed my family, St. Louis and the Cardinals.

As I said to the press when I came back to St. Louis: "They can take me away from the Cardinals, but they can never take the Cardinals away from me."

Turning Down a Fortune

When I made that decision to leave the Mets, I immediately called Don Grant. He said, "Would you give me a chance to change your mind? I'm at my winter home at Boca Raton, Florida. Can you come down here?"

I said, "Sure."

So I went down, and he made overtures. One of the things he said was, "If you stay, I can't give you a written guarantee, but I'd like to offer you a small piece of the club."

We never discussed how much because I said, "Don, that sounds generous. But I've made the decision to go home to my family and to the Cardinals, which was my hometown club."

Don said that he was sorry, but that he understood my decision.

I wanted to tell Mrs. Payson in person and not do it through another owner or by phone. I felt that I owed that to her because she had been so good to me. She had approved my hiring and a lot of the things I'd accomplished. So I made a date to meet her at her office in downtown Manhattan, on the same day I was coming back to St. Louis permanently.

It was December and I put in a hectic time driving from Shea to downtown and back to the airport. It was a clear, cold day and it wasn't snowing, but you can imagine the traffic with all the holiday shoppers in the city.

I can distinctly remember parking about 20 blocks from her office and looking for a cab and not finding one. So I walked the whole way.

When I finally got in to see Mrs. Payson, she was very gracious as always. I don't remember much about the conversation, but it was very personable back and forth, with a lot of respect, one for the other. I remember driving the company car back to Shea and getting my last ride from Shea to LaGuardia.

Leaving a Future Champ

I had no idea the Mets would win the World Series two years later. I'm not trying to pat myself on the back. But the big deal for Agee on December 15, 1967, was the only deal they made until after the middle of June in '69. That's when Johnny Murphy acquired Donn Clendenon, a platoon first baseman from Montreal.

It's really kind of unbelievable: He's the only player who came in after I left until they won the World Series. So I left the Mets in pretty good shape.

I guess it's kind of funny. I left the Cardinals in '64 right before they won a pennant and a World Series. I came back right after they won a pennant and a World Series in '67. Then we won a pennant in St. Louis my first year back in '68 but lost the World Series. And then the Mets won the pennant and the World Series in '69.

I didn't have any ties with the Mets like I had in '64 with the Cardinals. That's why when the Mets won in '69, I didn't have that kind of deep-seated, bittersweet feel that I had when I left St. Louis.

The decision had been made for me in '64, and the other decision I made for myself in '67.

But I think I'm better off not second-guessing myself. It's like a ballplayer having a bad day. You can't keep talking about it. If you want to be a great player and have a great career, you've got to forget about it and get back to work.

Which doesn't always come easy.

BING SAW SOMETHING IN ME

WHITEY HERZOG
REFLECTS ON BING DEVINE

In 1966, I coached third base for the Mets. I was only making about $12,000 or $12,500. I had come over from Oakland, and Charlie Finley wanted to bring me back. Bing got wind of it and said, "No, I'm not gonna let you go. What would it take for you to stay here as a special assistant to me?"

I told him $20,000.

He said, "You got it!"

So I became a special assistant to Bing Devine, and I ran the amateur draft for him.

At the end of the '67 season, Bing said, "You're really young and I know you'd still like to be in uniform. Why don't you switch jobs with Bob Scheffing and you take over our development program?"

So in September of '67, I took the job of player development director.

Bing Devine was the first guy who really saw something in me that nobody else did, as far as being in the front office instead of just coaching. He could just pick up the phone at one a.m. and call me. I'd be in Corpus Christi, scouting Burt Hooten, and he'd call and ask me about something. I'd give him an opinion, see, and he liked that.

As far as getting Tom Seaver in '66, our scouting director then was Nelson Burbrink, and he didn't like Seaver. He said he didn't throw hard enough. We finished ninth that year, one place out of last, but that was the first time we didn't finish in the cellar. Seaver was signed illegally by the Atlanta Braves and the commissioner found out and said they couldn't have him. His deal was for $40,000.

What would that have looked like to our fans, if we hadn't gone after him? Bing had to talk George Weiss into it, and that's how Bing ended up getting Seaver out of a hat.

I was out in Arizona in '67, scouting, and Bing called me. He said we were having our formal meetings down in Homestead, Florida, and he wanted me to be there.

He picked me up at the Miami Airport. We had signed Jerry Koosman for $1,000, and that was a story. Red Murff had gone down to Texas and offered him $1,500, but Koosman turned him down. Then Red went back and offered him $1,200, and Koosman turned him down again. After a while, Red went back a third time and offered him $1,000—and Koosman took it. He said, "If I don't take it, pretty soon I won't get nothing."

So Koosman was in our minor leagues, but most of our guys didn't like him. They didn't think he threw hard enough, either, just like they said about Seaver. Koosman didn't, but he had a nice delivery. I thought he might be able to pick up some speed as he matured.

So we were in the meeting, discussing players, and when we got to Koosman everybody said, "Release, release, release"—except Joe McDonald and Bing and me.

Joe said, "Hey, we just lent Koosman 50 dollars. And George Weiss is so tight, if we don't get that 50 dollars back, George is gonna can my ass!"

I know Bing said 500 dollars, but I clearly remember it was just 50 dollars. That's all it was.

Anyway, Clyde McCullough, the old catcher, was coaching one of our low minor league teams. And Clyde said, "I'll take him."

Clyde didn't take Koosman cause he liked him. He just took him for two weeks, till he could pay back the 50 bucks he owed us.

Well, Koosman pitched two shutouts for Clyde, and all of a sudden he's throwing 93, 94, 95 miles an hour. And that was how we kept Koosman.

I was there when Bing tried to make the Agee trade. We were at the winter meetings in Puerto Rico. Everybody wanted Bing to make the deal: Gil Hodges, Yogi Berra, Joe McDonald, me. But Donald Grant was there and he nixed it. Bing was putting a left-handed pitcher in the deal named Don Shaw, who later pitched for the Cardinals. Donald Grant said he saw Don Shaw strike out Hank Aaron one time, so he didn't want to give him up.

I told Grant, "I was at that game, and he did strike Hank Aaron out. But it was the second time in the inning that Aaron batted and he just wanted to get the hell out of there."

Grant didn't like that too much. And he nixed the deal anyhow.

That night, Bing and I and our wives were going out to eat. And Bing was still upset about not being able to make the Agee trade. I clearly remember that we were all walking. He and I were behind Mary and Mary Lou, and Bing said to me, "You know, I don't think they need a general manager here."

Just a couple of days later, he left and went back to St. Louis. But I think it was just a throwaway comment, because he was always grateful to the Mets for what they did for him.

He'd told me many times, "I was living in luck, because when I got fired by St. Louis in '64, the Mets came along before I even suffered loss of income."

Then when he got the chance to go back to St. Louis, where his family still was, and get his job back as GM, he couldn't turn that down.

Right after Bing went back to St. Louis, he called and asked me if I wanted to come along with him. And I said, "No, I think I'll stay here."

Seaver was already up with the big club in '67. But that summer in our minor league system, we had the darndest pitching staff that anybody ever had. Geez, we had some good young arms down there. We didn't have radar guns then, but I know I had three or four guys throwing the ball near 100 miles per hour. We had Koosman, Jon Matlack, Gary Gentry, Nolan Ryan, Tug McGraw, Jim McAndrew, Danny Frisella. And we had Bill Denehy, who Bing traded for Hodges, and we had Steve Renko, who we traded for Donn Clendenon in '69—the only guy on that team who wasn't in the organization when Bing left.

When the Mets won the World Series in '69, Seaver and Koosman never lost back-to-back games all year. They were our 1-2 guys, and Bing's the reason they were both there.

And we did make the Agee deal after Bing left, but Grant made us take Shaw out and put somebody else in.

I worked for two guys in my life, Bing Devine and Hank Peters, who are two of the most capable baseball executives of all time. They knew the game, could handle people, run meetings, do everything. I never understood why they didn't work in the commissioner's office when their careers as GMs were over. They could have given so much to baseball. That's something that Bing should have had 20 years ago, 30 years ago. I know, he wouldn't have done it anyhow because he didn't want to live in New York. But hell, the commissioner lives in Milwaukee now anyway.

So what's the difference?

Chapter 4

A Cardinal Is Hatched

A Reformed Sports Writer

When I was young, the first thing I wanted to be was a ballplayer. But I also thought I might pursue sports writing.

At Washington University I wrote for *Student Life*, the school paper. I had the title of sports editor. I pretty much wrote a weekly story. I might have done that a couple of years, my junior and senior year. I thought I wrote some pretty good columns. I also wrote for the *Watchman Advocate* in Clayton, a St. Louis suburb. I got that job when I met the publisher through my dad's office.

I took a special English course during my senior year of college. The professor's name was Webster. He only had 10 or 12 people in the class, and you had to turn in material in advance. We sat around a big table and everyone brought something they'd written.

You'd read it out loud, and then everyone would critique it, including the professor.

You had to write 50,000 words a year. I cheated some. I gave him some columns I'd written, probably for the *Watchman Advocate*. In other words, I took the easy way out. I was somewhat fearful that the professor would question the motivation. I'd copy them over, and he never did question them. Even though he knew where they came from.

As you can see, I wasn't a workaholic. To be honest with you, I shuffled through college. I was at Washington U. from 1933 to 1938. I stayed out of school a year in the middle of that period to work.

My dad was president of the Clayton Rotary Club. Ed Staples, publicity director for the Cardinals, spoke at a Rotary Club meeting. And afterward my dad talked to him, told him, with some pride, that I was writing a sports column, had a background in sports and had a sports-oriented mind. That led to Staples interviewing me for for the office job with the Cardinals. I brought a couple of sports columns with me from the *Advocate*, and I got into the publicity department, which is now public relations or media relations.

So I was a reformed sportswriter before I got hooked on professional baseball.

Signing on in '39

I first went to work for the Cardinals in 1939. I had just graduated from Washington University, where I played basketball and baseball.

I played basketball very well. I could shoot and was a real gunner. I'm in the Washington University sports Hall of Fame for basketball. I thought I played baseball very well, but I didn't. I'd been to some tryout camps with big-league clubs but never got signed.

When I joined the Cardinals, I helped around the office. I did little things like run the mimeograph machine to make copies, before they had the technology for Xerox machines.

Bob Broeg also worked in the office with me part-time. But he was going back to the University of Missouri in '39 to finish up before he joined the *Post-Dispatch* and went on to become sports editor.

I was still playing amateur baseball around the city. The various scouting personnel on the ball club knew me. They had worked me out at the old ballpark, Sportsman's Park, but wouldn't sign me. I had hopes that I could make the major leagues. Well, they were right and I was wrong!

But besides working in the office, I'd help pitch batting practice to the team at Sportsman's Park.

A Daring Debut

The '39 Cardinals had Joe "Ducky" Medwick, one of the greatest right-handed hitters of all time, and Johnny Mize, one of the best left-handed power hitters ever.

They're both in the Baseball Hall of Fame in Cooperstown, New York. And I was pitching batting practice to them, and Terry Moore and the rest of that Cardinal team.

Joe Medwick was one of my heroes, but he hated anyone who worked in the front office. He'd had a lot of contract troubles. It didn't matter that I was just an office boy. To him, anybody from the front office was the enemy. He'd try to line the ball back at any front office guy who was pitching batting practice. Back then, they didn't have a protective screen in front of the pitcher during batting practice.

Medwick would also take a shot at the pitchers, no matter who they were, if they didn't get the ball where he wanted it. He wanted to put on a show in batting practice, and the fans wanted him to put on a show, just like Mark McGwire did years later at Busch Stadium. Medwick would hit a dozen balls out of the park if he got his pitch. If he didn't, he'd line a shot back at the pitcher and yell, "Get the ball over and quit playing around!"

After my arm got tired from pitching, I'd go over to first base. I'd take throws from the infielders, who would have someone hit grounders to them between pitches. They didn't have a protective screen at first base then, either. You're in the line of fire for left-handed hitters, and you're talking about a left-handed hitter like Johnny Mize pulling the ball down the line.

One time in 1940 I was playing first base and somebody, I don't know if it was Mize, ripped a ball down to first. It hit me on the shin and I went down.

As people often say about me, the last thing I ever want is attention, no matter what I'm doing. But I had a hard time getting back up from that shot. I finally kind of limped off and went into the clubhouse.

Marty Marion, our shortstop, came all the way in from the field after me. He said, "I saw you get hit. I know you got hit hard. And I know you got hurt."

He wanted me to get checked out, but I said, "Don't tell anybody."

Marty Marion was the first ballplayer who ever befriended me. And we're still friends today. For the record, I've said for years that Marion should be in the Baseball Hall of Fame in Cooperstown. And I still believe that.

Not Ducky

Even though Medwick didn't like front office people, he never made it a major issue. I'd talk to him when I saw him in the locker room.

One time, I was down there using the shower. Medwick came into the locker room, grumbling that he didn't feel well that day. I'd pitched batting practice that day, but not to him.

When he saw me he said, "It's a good thing you didn't pitch to me today. I might just have taken some good shots at you!"

He was ranting and raving, so I got out of there. Terry Moore followed me out of there and said, "Don't pay any attention to him. He's just popping off. He didn't mean it."

Terry was a nice guy. He was just trying to make sure my feelings weren't hurt. But it didn't bother me. I didn't worry about that kind of stuff.

I think about all of that that now, and I wonder: Could I really have had so little sense as to pitch batting practice or play first base with those kinds of hitters up there? But I was eager back in those days, and it just didn't register.

Head Count

When I was working as an office boy for the Cardinals in 1939 and 1940, I'd get the attendance from the ticket manager for every game at Sportsman's Park. He'd write the number down on a little scrap of paper. Not a full sheet, just a scrap. And I'd take that to Sam Breadon, the owner, who was always sitting in his box next to the dugout. I'd show it to him, and I'd cup the paper in my hands so nobody else could see it.

Say the attendance was 7,000. He'd say, "Let's make it 12,000."

I'd have another piece of paper, and I'd write down 12,579 or whatever number he told me. Then I'd take it up and show it to J. Roy Stockton sitting in the middle of the press box. He was the old writer for the *Post-Dispatch*, kind of the senior member of the press corps. He'd take a look at it and pass it around to the rest of the writers.

When the Browns played the first night game at home, they had an announced crowd of something like 20,000 at Sportsman's Park. About a week or 10 days later, the Cardinals played their first night game at home. We ended up with a considerably smaller crowd in Sportsman's Park than the Browns had had during their game. But when I went took the actual attendance for approval, Sam upped the figure so that it was more than the Browns'.

I took the paper to Stockton in the press box. He looked at it and said, "Hey, what are guys trying to put over? Who are you kidding?"

Stockton knew full well I didn't have anything to do with it. I was just a kid out of college. But I didn't know what to say, so I just left and started to take the paper back to Breadon.

When I got under the stands I ran into Bill Walsingham. He was assistant to the president and he was also Breadon's nephew. Bill asked me where I was going, so I told him what happened.

He said, "We've got to do something about that."

The park only held about 30,000 people. If we drew more than the Browns, that meant it was almost full. In a small park like that, you couldn't juggle attendance figures by 10,000 and get away with it.

So we went back to Breadon together and Bill said, "We've got a problem. We can't do the attendance this way."

Breadon agreed. So he and Bill came up with a figure that was under what the Browns had, but still more than what we had in the park.

I took that new figure back up to the press box and gave it to Stockton. He looked at it and said, "What happened?"

I said, "Well, they had a miscount at the ticket office."

Stockton gave me a funny look, and then he passed the paper around the press box. And I got out of there.

So early on I was asked to cover up for an owner. Isn't it amazing how you remember something like that more than 60 years later? I guess maybe because it wasn't the last time I had to cover for an owner!

Sam's Club

Over the ticket offices at the main entrance to the old Sportsman's Park were the baseball offices for the Browns and Cardinals. You had to walk up a big flight of stairs to get to the office level. We each had our own set of stairs. The Browns were on the east end of the executive offices, and we were on the west end. There was a walkway from one office to the other, and it was open. We were competitors, true, but let's face it: There were some business relations that they could handle one for the other, like public relations.

The ticket windows were on Dodier Street, right across from Carter Carburetor.

Now picture this. It was summer in St. Louis. The heat was really oppressive. We were all sweating to beat heck. Joe Mathes, who ran the minor leagues for us, was sitting there with his collar open—like all the rest of us working in the Cardinals office. Joe was a real big man, and he had his handkerchief on his head to soak up the perspiration.

We had all our windows open up in the offices to try to get a little air in. There was probably more heat coming in than going out. And across the street, Carter's is running its machines and making all this noise.

I can recall one day when Joe Mathes was sitting in his office and had some business to see about with the Browns. He walked through to their offices and took care of whatever he had to do.

Then Joe came back and walked up to Mr. Breadon's office. The door was open. No doors were ever closed up there. And Mr. Breadon was sitting at his desk. He had his collar open, sweating profusely, with all this noise from the carburetor company coming in the window.

Joe was all excited. He said, "Mr. Breadon! I've just been over to the Browns' office, and boy it's wonderful! They've got *air conditioning!*"

Mr. Breadon just looked up at him and said, "That's right...And we've got the *ball club.*"

That stopped the conversation.

Since we won the World Series in 1926, the Cards were always winning, or competitive. And the Browns always lost, except for '44 when they played the Cardinals in the World Series.

The Browns had the air conditioning. But we had the ball club.

I never forgot that.

A MAN OF MANY FRIENDS

MARTY MARION REFLECTS ON BING DEVINE

Bing is so popular in baseball.

I told him years ago, "You ought to do a book. You've got more to write about than anybody I know. You've had so many important positions. You know everybody in baseball. Everybody likes you."

You know, he was the first person I saw when I came to St. Louis in 1940. He befriended me right away. I didn't know his position up there with the Cardinals. He was in the office, I knew that. But Bing loved to be on the field. He loved being around the players.

One time he got hit with a line drive, and I told him he wasn't supposed to be on the field! But he kept going out there. He got hit pretty good that time and wanted to come back out right away, but I wouldn't let him do that.

That was 60 years ago, but you know what? Some things stick in your mind. Probably because Bing always brings it up!

He'll say, "Remember when I was taking infield during batting practice, and I got hit by that ball?"

And I say, "I sure do."

I remember Joe Medwick being rough on him. Medwick had a very bad reputation, not only with Bing but with anybody who came along. Joe would hit the ball back at the pitcher in batting practice if he didn't like where the ball was pitched. And Joe could handle a bat. He could hit the ball where he wanted to.

The Gas House Gang was out of there in the '40s, by the time I got to the Cardinals. The Gas House Gang was there in the '30s, and Medwick was a part of them. That was a rough bunch, and Medwick was hard-nosed.

Bing was not forward, that's for sure. He was just a nice friend. He was a kid in the office and I was ballplayer, but I was just a kid myself. I was already married when I got to St. Louis. Bing wasn't. But he had a girlfriend then, and I used to go out with Bing on dates, me and my wife and Bing and his girlfriend.

Then he went to Johnson City, Tennessee, as an executive, and that's where he met Mary. They got married and had a wonderful family. We've been friends all these years. My wife and Mary, they still talk every day on the phone.

The thing about Bing is that he always had a job. When the Cardinals let him go the first time, he went to the Mets and became president. He worked for a lot of teams. I never worked for him, but I know everybody who works for him loves him.

Anything the Cardinals wanted him to do, Bing did it. He's a company man. He's had a long, long career. And he's no spring chicken. I'm 87, and he's a little bit older than I am.

He still scouts for the Cardinals. I can't believe it. And he's 88 years old! That speaks for itself, buddy, that he's still working.

He's had a fabulous career. And I can't think of a better person to call if you have a question about baseball. Everybody leans on Bing for information, even today. Bing is number one for information. He is never at a loss for words.

And he was always a guy you could depend on, if you needed anything or asked for anything. If it was in his power to do it, he'd do it for you. Like getting you World Series tickets.

He is a man of many friends. And I guess that's about the best thing you can say about anybody.

Chapter 5

Minor Successes

Beating the Bushes

In '41, I went to our Cardinals farm club in Johnson City, Tennessee, as the business manager. I wound up playing second base there under amazing circumstances.

When World War II started, the Cardinals' front office told me they were running out of players. They were all being drafted into the service. But I had a high draft number, so I didn't get called up right away.

So the Cardinals told me, "If you run low on players at your position"—which was second base—"sign yourself to a contract and put yourself in the field."

And that's what I ended up doing.

Scouting a Sweetheart

The best thing about Johnson City was that I met my wife, Mary, there. She worked in a jewelry store in "downtown" Johnson City, which had a population of about 25,000 people. The train came through there regularly and stopped traffic in the middle of downtown when it dropped off passengers.

We had a second baseman in Johnson City named Mickey Cochrane. He wasn't the famous catcher. His first name wasn't really Mickey, but everyone called him that. He was dating Mary before I got there, and then we got rid of him.

I didn't make trades then at that level, Class D. They all came out of the St. Louis office. That's why I was really the business manager, rather than a traditional general manager. But I tell people I traded him so I could play second base and date Mary. Or date Mary and play second base, which is the order if she's listening!

Anyway, Mary saw me play, and I guess she felt sorry for me. She married me after that '41 season on October 25th. Our honeymoon trip was spent traveling to Fresno, California, to take over the Class C minor league club there.

We've been married 62 years now. So I guess she got over Mickey Cochrane.

Playing with Fire

At Johnson City, I was general manager, business manager, groundskeeper, and second baseman. And I was courting my wife. All at the same time.

I had to help open the ballpark. I used to go out and get the ticket sellers set up with their change before the game. Then I'd go into the clubhouse and put on a uniform and go out and take infield practice. I never had time to take batting practice, but that wasn't the reason I couldn't hit. I couldn't hit anyway, regardless of how much batting practice I took.

If it rained and the field was still wet, you'd put gasoline on it and light it. That's the way we used to dry the infields back then. We used to do that in the big leagues, too, years ago. One time in Johnson City, I was drying the infield and I burned myself into the middle of a circle of fire. The flames were all around me, but there were a few places where you could get through, and I was able to escape.

How does something like that happen? We weren't very smart, that's how.

Good Field, No Hit

Johnny Morrow was the shortstop and the manager at Johnson City. Toward the end of the year, the Cardinals had to get him out of there because he had too many fights with umpires. But he was the manager when I played second base.

I was actually a pretty good fielder. But I used to tell people, "I was so bad at bat, I'm the only hitter I ever knew that the manager had a bunt sign for with two out, two strikes and nobody on base!"

Actually, Johnny Morrow would tell me, "I ought to get you started by giving you the bunt sign."

People say I'm honest with them, which is flattering. But I got caught one time bending the truth. A guy was doing an article on me a few years ago, and I told him I hit .250 at Johnson City.

A couple days later he called me back and said, "I've got a record book, and you didn't even hit .150!"

I said, "If you hit as bad as I did, wouldn't you say you hit .250 if you thought nobody would look it up?"

Actually, I hit .118 in 27 games in '41. And that was the end of my career as a professional baseball player.

The Truth Hurt

They say I'm shy about talking about my sports life, but I could play basketball. That was my best sport.

I played at Washington University in St. Louis and made their Hall of Fame. We're going back to ancient history in basketball here! I remember we played Oklahoma A&M, which is now Oklahoma State, and the score was something like 26-13. That was a typical score. I was still taking two-handed set shots then.

I played semipro basketball around St. Louis after college. And I played basketball for the Naval Air Station in Kaneohe Bay in Hawaii during World War II.

All along I tried to play baseball, but the scouts were right. I couldn't. I hear guys all the time who say, "I think I could have played in the big leagues if I got the chance." I might be saying the same thing if I hadn't gotten to play second base there at Johnson City.

I found out I couldn't play. And here's why: I had a fear of the pitched ball. It was built into me. If you have that fear, you can't hit.

We didn't have batting helmets back then. But even with helmets, that's still the biggest thing for young players' hitting—fear of the ball.

Working at Curtiss Wright

In between leaving pro baseball and going into the navy for World War II, I worked for Curtiss Wright in St. Louis for about a year. They were a defense contractor out at Lambert Field. I had applied for officer training and was accepted, but they delayed my active duty for some time.

I didn't know how long it would be before I left, so I talked to Sam Breadon, who owned the Cardinals then. I asked him what my future with the ball club was, and he said he didn't know. He didn't know how many minor league clubs would be operating, because we didn't know how many ballplayers would be available with the military draft going on.

I had a high draft number, so I knew I'd be one of the last people called up. As the best choice I could make, rather than have them send me wherever they wanted to send me, I wanted to have some kind of choice. So I enlisted in the navy.

Sam told me, "Since you're going into the navy eventually, it would be helpful if you found something in the meantime outside of baseball. If you don't, we'll find something for you—but I don't know what."

I knew a coach at St. Charles High School, Coach Dueringer. We had a pretty good acquaintance from my playing amateur ball around town. I gave him my story and told him I would benefit from some kind of war plant job. He left coaching to join the war plant at Curtis-Wright, and he led the recreation department out there. They had a very big aviation company, with their headquarters out at Lambert Field. He recommended that I get an interview.

What did I know about factories or machines? But I got hired anyway. I did a work-time study for the company. I studied the work ethic of the employees in the various departments. I'd talk to them and get some idea of improving the time element of their jobs, to get things done quicker.

So the work I did in the plant on that basis was an excuse for me to play on the company baseball and basketball teams. They had a really big war plant league back then. And you know who coached the baseball team and played first base? George Silvey. He was a minor league scouting director with the Cardinals, a pretty big man with scouting and player development back then.

Mary and I lived in an apartment down on Plymouth Avenue at the time. I remember working various shifts during the day. I can remember that late-night shift was a murder. You went in at midnight and got off at eight o'clock in the morning.

I was there about nine months or a year. I was in the navy but not yet assigned anywhere. So I played second base for Curtiss Wright.

I began to realize early in my amateur baseball career that I wasn't going to hit much. So I thought I'd try to pitch. But I found out I wasn't going to pitch much, either.

Hello, Columbus

When I came back from the war, in 1946 and '47, I was general manager of the Cardinals' Class A team in Columbus, Georgia.

Spec Richardson was a longtime resident of Columbus, Georgia, and he was our concessionaire. That's how he got his start in baseball. He went on to become a big-league general manager, and I ended up scouting for him when he was with San Francisco.

The park in Columbus was not in the best part of town. Once while I was a on a trip, somebody shot through the office at night. Nobody was in there, but somebody shot a hole in the wall with a shotgun.

The police decided somebody might not have known I was gone. They were fearful that someone was gunning for me. Our office was up over the ticket windows. You got up there by going up a small flight of stairs. During games, they gave me a policeman to guard the steps.

We had a very elderly guy as the night watchman, Mr. Brooks. He was as old as I am now—in other words, in his upper 80s. Mr. Brooks sat there in the office at night with a shotgun. And one night, he knocked the gun over and it went off. The bullet hit him in the leg.

He called me up at home and said, "Bing, this is Mister Brooks."

I said, "Yessss…"

He said, "I just shot myself."

The poor guy was sitting there with a bullet in him.

It sounds funny now, but he was in a lot of pain. That was life in the minor leagues back then.

Joe Wouldn't Go Up

Joe Cunningham was the first baseman at Rochester when I was the general manager there in 1954.

He'd been up with the Cardinals, came back to Triple A in Rochester, and then the Cardinals wanted him back up. All in the same season.

I called him in to the office and said, "I've got some good news. You're going up to St. Louis."

He was crestfallen. I couldn't believe it.

He said, "What? Why?"

I said, "Because they need you."

Joe said, "I don't want to go."

Then it was my turn. I said, "What? Why? You're going to the big leagues!"

Apparently he wasn't happy about how they sent him down before. And he really did not want to go back.

I told him, "Look, they need you. They want you. And they're the boss."

He said, "Well, talk to them and see what you can do about it."

I said, "Okay, I'll talk to them, but I can tell you now that you'll have to go."

So I did what he asked me. I remember calling the Cardinals and telling them, "He doesn't want to come."

And of course they wanted him anyway. I said, "Well, he's coming up under protest!"

But he went.

And that was a first for me with players moving through the organization.

Send 'em down? Sure, I had some crybabies who were unhappy about that, having to go back to the minors. But send 'em up? Joe's the only one I ever met who didn't want to get promoted to the big leagues.

He wound up playing for the Cardinals through most of the '50s, and he's been working in their front office for years.

So it's a good thing he had a change of heart back there in Rochester.

Ed Wouldn't Go Down

There was a guy, Ed Mickelson, who went to University City High after I did and also played first base at Rochester when I was the general manager.

I called Mickelson into my office one time to tell him we were sending him down to a lower level. And he threatened me.

He said, "I'm not going. You can't do this. And you better not try!"

He didn't use force, but he threatened force. He's a big guy and he was intimidating. I really was intimidated. But I sent him down anyway. And he finally went.

He wound up playing briefly with the Cardinals, Cubs and Browns. In fact, he drove in the last run in Browns history before they moved to Baltimore and became the Orioles.

He later became a coach at U. City High. One of his players there was a left-handed pitcher named Kenny Holtzman, who went on to get five World Series rings with the A's and Yankees.

But those were the two extremes: Mickelson on the one side and Cunningham on the other.

Wally Never Showed Up

In the spring of '54, a young outfielder named Wally Moon was supposed to report to Daytona, where Rochester had camp. Instead, he went to the big-league camp at St. Pete with the Cardinals.

Eddie Stanky was managing the Cardinals then. He kept Moon, and Moon wound up taking Enos Slaughter's job, hitting over .300 and winning Rookie of the Year in the National League.

I was the general manager with Rochester. Nobody told us he wasn't coming to camp with us. He said he went to that big-league camp by mistake—his own. Which I thought was phony.

I remember thinking, "This can't be by accident, because Moon's a smart guy."

He proved that a few years later when we traded him to the Dodgers. He's the one who made the adjustment to the Coliseum in L.A., hitting those home runs to the opposite field over that short fence in left field.

All I know is, we never saw him like we were supposed to in '54. Whether it was an honest mistake or not, that's another example of something I never saw before or since.

Peggy's Filing System

My secretary at Rochester was named Peggy. She was a good secretary, but she was bipolar, I guess you'd say now. She was a worker, but she worked in the extreme. She worked late all the time. I'd tell her to go home, but you couldn't run her off. She'd be there all day and then all through the ballgame.

I didn't force her to work like that. She just loved it. But we finally had to let her go because it was getting the best of her. She couldn't deal with it physically any more. After she left, we found out that a lot of the files were missing. Contracts and things like that, which we really needed.

Her husband's name was Dick. When I called her to ask about the missing files, she said, "I've got them here at home, but Dick doesn't like what you did to me. Dick said I shouldn't see you because we'll get in a fight. So I'm not going to bring them back."

I said I'd come over to get them, and she said okay. But I brought along Mary, my wife, because I didn't want to go over there by myself without a witness.

We drove over there, and there were files on the porch. All over the porch. Peggy had brought them all home through the years and had never taken them back. There were so many files that they almost filled the car.

I never had anything like that happen before or since, either.

Hiring Jack Buck the First Time

In the early '50s, the Cardinals had two Triple A farm clubs. One was in Rochester, New York, and the other was in Columbus, Ohio. They really had three that they treated at the top level, counting the one they had in Houston.

I was the general manager in Rochester from 1949 to 1955. My last years there, the Columbus general manager was a fellow named Al Banister. He was a longtime Cardinals minor-league executive.

After the '52 season, I think somewhere around November or December, Al called me in Rochester and said, "I wonder how your radio broadcasts are setting up?"

It just so happened, completely by accident, that we had an opening. Our radio guy had been Eddie Williams, a local guy. He lived in Rochester and did the games for a short while. I didn't think he was very good, so I let him go. Eddie had a following because he lived in town, and they had a half-baked demonstration, picketing us. As I recall, it was the people from his neighborhood. It wasn't a violent thing. But it was kind of troublesome. There was a ripple of dissatisfaction. So I said to Al, "We just made a change, but we haven't hired anybody yet. Do you have anybody to recommend?"

He said, "Yeah, we've got a play-by-play man and we like him, but we're not going to be able to keep him. We just don't have the interest here in a radio sponsor. I don't know if we'll even have a broadcast next year.

"So I'd like to recommend a man named Jack Buck."

To be honest, I don't remember that the name hit me real big. I said that I wanted to talk to a couple people about him, but that we were considering other people, too.

So Jack Buck came up and auditioned and met the people from the sponsor, a local brewery there in Rochester. And I hired him right away. The Cardinals didn't know anything about it. Dick Meyer was my boss back in St. Louis, and I told Dick almost everything I was doing with the club. But things like the radio announcer you handled yourself in the minor leagues.

I knew there wasn't going to be a problem with this decision. There was no way in the world you couldn't have been impressed by Jack Buck, even back then. He was a very young man, but he was vintage Jack Buck. The Jack Buck you got to know here in St. Louis was the Jack Buck we got to know immediately in Rochester, 50 years ago.

He was an individual who could find a touch of humor in everything. He was an outstanding speaker. He had an exceptional radio and television voice, although there wasn't much television work then. I don't think he was saying "That's a winner!" after we won a game back then. I think that was a later development when he got to St. Louis. But he had all the attributes in Rochester. And he didn't learn them. He just had them.

So Jack's first season in Rochester was in '53. We didn't send our broadcasters on the road, which wasn't very unusual in those days. It was too expensive to justify for the number of people listening in. Jack would sit back in the studio in Rochester, recreating the games from the reports on the Western Union ticker. And he was outstanding at that. They'd have crowd noise in the background on tape. He made you feel that he was there and that you were there.

But he didn't just make you feel you were at the game. More importantly, he'd make you *wish* you were at the game. And he had a way of making a bad game sound good.

I heard him a lot because I didn't usually go on the road, either. I would just go to Syracuse and Buffalo, the cities that were closest to us in the International League. I would hear him at home games a lot, too. I'd have to go to the office to do something, and I'd have the broadcast on.

It was just obvious that Jack Buck had what made broadcasters the best. He had a knowledge of the game, and he could paint a picture of the game on radio and later on television. Jack not only described the game, he made a point of learning the players' personalities. All the players on all the teams, not just ours.

As I said about a lot of great ballplayers, he was a talent who worked at his trade.

When we hired him I remember thinking, "What a coincidence! We just happened to have an opening." I didn't know that we were getting a gem of all broadcasters. So credit Al Banister for making that call to me.

Hiring Jack Buck a Second Time

A year after we brought Jack Buck to Rochester, I was on the phone with Dick Meyer from Anheuser-Busch. The brewery had bought the Cardinals in '53. And if they were going to enter the picture as an owner, they wanted their own broadcast.

Harry Caray was established as the play-by-play announcer. But Dick called me up and said, "As a new sponsor of the Cardinals' broadcast, which we now own, we're looking for a new voice to join Harry Caray. We want to add a different flavor to the broadcast."

Now, Dick Meyer had been up to Rochester the previous season. I'm sure he met Buck then. I'm sure he heard me talk about Buck. And he probably heard the broadcast with Buck.

My point is, Dick knew how good Jack Buck was. But Dick asked me, "Do you think it would be worth our while to consider him and interview him?"

I said, "Yes, of course!"

I didn't know what the competition would be, who else they were considering for the job. But I didn't have any question that he'd be impressive.

That phone call from Dick Meyer led to the marketing people at the brewery bringing Jack Buck in to St. Louis for a meeting. As you know, to meet him is to like him and actually to love him…as a voice, as a personality and as a person. What you saw with Jack Buck was what you would get all the time.

And that led to the career in St. Louis that we all admired. But it all goes back to the luck of the draw. You have Al Banister being willing, over there in Columbus, to make a call to me in Rochester about an announcer. That's a really small item in the minor leagues. And then you have the luck of us needing an announcer in Rochester when Al called. And then me having the good luck to hire him. And then the luck of the Cardinals being sold and needing someone to work with Harry Caray.

Friend and Neighbor

It was hard to see Jack Buck leave Rochester, even though I was happy that he'd gotten the Cardinals job.

At the minor league level, the broadcaster was part of the team. The whole operation was so small, it was like a family. My wife Mary and I really got to know Jack and his first wife Alice and the rest of his family.

When Jack first got to St. Louis in '54, he lived on Elizabeth Street on The Hill. Yogi Berra and Joe Garagiola had grown up on Elizabeth Street, at the other end of the block, before they'd gone off to catch in the big leagues.

The next year, after the '55 season, Dick Meyer brought me to the Cardinals as assistant general manager to Frank Lane. So Jack beat us to St. Louis. But we beat him to the neighborhood.

I came up right away and bought this house in Ladue where we still live, and I actually bought it without Mary ever seeing it. Not many wives trust their husbands to buy a house sight unseen.

But we had three young daughters, and the youngest was just six months old. It wasn't convenient for Mary to make the trip from Rochester to pick a house.

She told me, "You grew up in St. Louis. You know it better than I do. Just get one near a school."

We wound up close enough to the high school that the girls could walk to it.

A year or two after we moved in, Jack Buck bought a lot at the other end of the development and built a house. I'm sure our being here had some effect on him. He'd been to our house socially.

And after he moved in, we got even closer to him and his family. I'd go to work early. He'd by driving by, going to whatever his duty was that day, and Mary would be at the breakfast room table, having a cup of coffee, and occasionally he'd stop in and have a cup of coffee with her. That's how close our families were.

Jack lived in the subdivision for 10 or 12 years, I guess, until he and Alice got divorced. We remained very close to him all these years, after he married Carole. And we remained close to Alice, too.

To me, Jack Buck was not only an announcer. He was a best friend.

A Keane Manager

The way the Cardinals got Jack Buck is also the way they got Johnny Keane as the manager. He was my manager at Rochester, but I didn't really bring him in when I was the general manager there.

The key to hiring managers back then in the Cardinals farm system was Joe Mathes. He ran their minor-league system. The whole operation wasn't streamlined and sophisticated as it is now. Joe basically moved the players up and down and hired the managers by himself.

So Johnny Keane and I inherited each other in Rochester. I was lucky to get him, just as I was with Jack Buck. But once I got both of those guys, I knew what to do with them!

As a person, Keane impressed me as Stan Musial did. I'm not talking about hitting or anything to do with playing baseball in the field. I'm talking about basic traits as a person. And John Keane was a nice man. Both Keane and Musial had a great work ethic, too. And it always seems to come back to that.

As a baseball man and as a manager, I got to know Keane well in Rochester. He was a professional. He knew his way around. He knew how to judge talent, and how to run a ballgame, and how to get along with minor league personnel. As a minor league manager, it's important to get along with your personnel. You don't have much help down there.

During a ballgame, he knew how to get the most from his personnel. And most of all, for a minor league manager, he knew how to develop his personnel for the big leagues.

I was at Rochester from '49 to '55, and we made the playoffs all six years I was there. We made it three years under Johnny Keane and then three more with Harry Walker.

Walker was a playing manager. He sure could talk and he was a nice man, too. Harry had a lot of things going for him, but he wasn't the same sweet kind of personality that Johnny Keane was.

See, as I mentioned, it was a family relationship at the minor league level. But the general manager and the manager work even more closely together.

I didn't know that Johnny Keane and I would be working together again in St. Louis. But it took almost 10 years for that to happen.

A Long Apprenticeship

I wound up hitting almost every level of minor league ball before I made it to the big leagues as an executive.

Johnson City, where I started in '41, was in the Class D Appalachian League. The next year I went to Fresno in the Class C California League. We couldn't play night ball in Fresno because of blackouts on the West Coast, due to the threat of air attacks by the Japanese. So the league folded after about half a season. For the rest of that '42 season the Cardinals sent me to Decatur, Illinois, which was in the Three I League in Class B.

After that, I left the Cardinals' organization and joined the navy. When I returned to the Cardinals, all of my qualifications from the lower leagues—Classes D, C and B—ended up landing me a spot in A ball. The Cardinals sent me to Columbus, Georgia. Then in '49, I finally moved up to Triple A for six years in Rochester.

Every time I went to one of these new teams and communities, I learned something from somebody. Usually from the manager, but sometimes from a veteran reporter covering the team.

In Fresno, the manager was Lou Scoffic, an ex-outfielder who had a cup of coffee with the Cardinals in '36.

In Decatur, the manager was Tony Kaufmann, a former major league pitcher. He was a legend, really. I remembered when he played in the big leagues with the Cardinals and a couple of other teams, and he'd been through the mill in the minor leagues. The reporter with the Decatur newspaper was Howard Millard, who was quite a bit older than me and had been around the block a time or two.

On those three teams, the only manager close to me in age was Johnny Morrow in Johnson City. He played shortstop while I played second, and I use the phrase "played second" loosely.

But at every level, I learned to pick up things, from the managers in particular. How to handle things, and more importantly, how not to handle things: players, games, off-the-field situations.

I also confirmed my belief that it was easy to get irritated with a media person—newspaper, radio and later on, television—but that it was best to try to avoid getting at cross-purposes with anyone.

The higher you went in the minors, the more you ran into people who had extensive experience, and who could pass on even more knowledge. I was smart enough or lucky enough to take advantage of what they all knew—or didn't know. People in baseball have pretty good memories, and they like to talk. I would listen to their stories and I couldn't help but learn from them. Something was bound to rub off. By the time I got to Triple A, I was working with managers like Johnny Keane and Harry Walker—great baseball men—and I was really beginning my education.

I believe that you learn something every day, good and bad, from somebody. A lot of people don't even realize they're learning something, but they are. If you do realize it, you pay particular attention to what and where and how you're learning. You continue to cultivate that knowledge. Even after you're lucky enough to reach the big leagues.

FALLING FOR A CARDINAL

MARY DEVINE
REFLECTS ON BING DEVINE

To say this life of baseball has been easy would be a lie. But that's not to say I haven't loved it, because I have … mostly, anyway!

When I think way back to the first time I laid my eyes on that handsome second baseman for the Johnson City Cardinals—and fell for him right away—I could never have imagined that our lives would be powered by this game of baseball.

We made a living from it. We moved our family because of the opportunities it held. Our social lives were shaped around it. And our family vacations were spent at its Florida springtime training event.

If given the opportunity, would I have chosen a different type of life for our three girls and me? I honestly don't have any idea, because I don't know anything else.

To Bing, I just want to say: You've been my husband for 62 years now. Jokingly throughout the years, we've both said that the reason we stayed happily married for so long was because this game of baseball kept us apart for at least half of that time.

Your scouting trips. Your months away at spring training. Your World Series jaunts. Those three years you spent in New York with the Mets. Even your trip to Japan when the Cardinals played the Japanese teams, and to Vietnam to "entertain" the troops.

We missed you, the girls and I, but we were proud of you.

You always set an example of hard work, ethical business practices, risk taking and doing what you loved. And we knew that in many ways you were doing it for us, to make sure we had a comfortable lifestyle.

So has this life of baseball been easy? Heck no!

But has it been good? Definitely yes!

And when I think back to the first time I saw that handsome second baseman for the Johnson City Cardinals … I'm glad I fell.

Chapter 6

A Big-League GM

Keeping Stan the Man

Dick Meyer wanted to bring me up from Rochester to be general manager in 1956, and I came up expecting to get that job. But some big Anheuser-Busch stockholder from the Chicago area who was a fan told Mr. Busch, "You ought to get Frank Lane. He's available." And that's what Mr. Busch did. Frank Lane was the general manager in St. Louis in 1956 and 1957, and I was his assistant until I got promoted to GM on November 12, 1957.

During Lane's first season, he traded Red Schoendienst. Then, before the '57 season, Lane tried to trade Stan Musial. He wanted to send Musial back to Pittsburgh, his hometown. I don't remember who we were getting in return.

I've heard the rumors since then that Lane wanted to send Musial to Philadelphia for Robin Roberts. Going back to my days with Lane, I remember some discussion about Robin Roberts. I don't remember Musial's name being mentioned, but Roberts was a big name. He was a Hall of Fame pitcher. You were going to have to deal a big name back to get a guy like him, so it's extremely possible that Musial might have been discussed.

If he was, I wasn't told about it. Which was not that unusual. There's no question that Frank had a lot of discussions that I didn't know about. And there's no way I could be involved in every trade discussion he had. Every time Frank picked up the phone, it could have been a potential deal. He didn't have to be close to the trade deadline to make a trade.

So my only memory of a Musial deal was with Pittsburgh, but I can't tell you for whom we were dealing. And I can't tell you that I was the one who stopped it. I know I didn't like it, but I was only Lane's assistant. I couldn't stop it.

The guy who did halt the trade was Al Fleishman, who was with the public relations firm Fleishman Hillard. He was the PR man for Gussie Busch at the brewery and at the ball club, and Mr. Busch really leaned on him.

Al found out somehow that Lane was working on a deal involving Musial. He might have heard from somebody on the ball club, like Jim Toomey, who was in the publicity office. Or it might have been Lane himself. He liked to tell people about his trades.

But when Al Fleishman got word of it, Al said to me, "Do you like it?" And I said, "No!"

At this point, Lane had never received a negative reaction to his deals from Mr. Busch. I'm sure Al thought that trading Musial was bad for the ball club. In addition to that, Al was a pretty sharp public relations man. He had a feeling that from a PR standpoint, as well as a personal viewpoint, trading Musial would be a big mistake.

Then Al said to Dick Meyer, "Hey, Lane's trying to break up the whole club. We've got to get the boss to stop him."

Dick Meyer was Gussie Busch's right-hand man at the brewery. When Dick told Busch about it, Busch said, "Tell Lane the deal's off!"

My memory is that deal was killed when Lane was driving to spring training in Florida. Lane drove a flashy car, a big convertible. He loved to drive with the top down to let the wind and sun hit his face. He loved to burn.

I stayed here in St. Louis as the interim GM. Lane didn't need me down there. Dick Meyer told me later that he got a call through to Lane at the hotel and said, "You're not trading Musial. Anywhere."

Lane, I'm sure, was crestfallen. He lived through his deals. And he didn't like anyone telling him what he could and couldn't do.

That was the beginning of the end for him as general manager here. It shook him up. There's no question in my mind that from then on, Lane had a feeling that they wanted to know what he was going to do and how he was going to do it.

And then he was gone.

Goodbye to Trader Lane

I'm sure Al Fleishman talked to Musial about the near trade. And I'm sure Musial wasn't surprised that it might have happened, knowing Frank Lane and his reputation.

Aside from thinking it helped the club, I think it served a purpose for Lane personally, too. He was used to having his stamp on the club. Guys like Musial and Schoendienst were the big guys— the guys getting a lot of attention. I think that disappointed Lane. He liked being Trader Lane. He realized that the more flair present, the better it was for him. And he didn't want to lose that. But mostly, he really did love making deals.

After he left St. Louis, he went to Cleveland and wound up trading managers with Detroit. Nobody else has ever done that.

If Frank Lane didn't make a deal in a month, he'd be nasty, just like a smoker who needed a cigarette.

Learning from the Trader

Before Frank Lane left the Cardinals, he told me, "I've got a deal with the Phillies—Ken Boyer for Richie Ashburn.

I told them it's going to be up to Bing Devine. They understand that you're taking over as general manager, and I can't force this deal on you."

And I didn't do it. I wasn't trading Ken Boyer, even though Ashburn eventually made the Hall of Fame.

Boyer came to us as a pitcher in Rochester in '50. He was signed as a pitcher because he had such a good arm. The year before, he hit .455 at Lebanon and was also 5-1 as a pitcher. He was an outfielder back then. We took a long look at him in spring training. I liked him. He was a competitor.

Schoendienst, Musial, Boyer…I wouldn't have traded any of them.

But I want to emphasize that I liked Frank Lane personally. I liked working for him. He was a baseball man. As I've said before, I saw what it meant not to close your mind to making deals. Working for him made me much more aggressive as a general manager.

That was important for my career. Even talking about dealing Stan Musial, which I didn't want to do, taught me something: You shouldn't ignore the possibility of doing anything, making any kind of move. When someone calls with a deal, no matter what it is, at least listen to it.

I think I would have been a conservative worrier if I hadn't worked for Frank Lane. I learned not to be a "scaredy-cat."

That's not to say I didn't make deals where I said, "I hope this works out…"

But if Frank Lane ever worried about a deal, I didn't sense it. He knew that nobody can ever guarantee that a deal's going to be that good, no matter how good it seems.

You've just got to do what you've got to do.

Acquiring Curt Flood

My first deal as a big-league general manager came at the winter meetings in 1957. I remember it distinctly.

At the winter meetings, you have discussions round the clock with the other general managers in the hotel. We had one such conversation with Gabe Paul, who was the Cincinnati GM.

There was not one player we were specifically seeking. Then this deal developed that we thought we could make. After Gabe and I first talked about it, I remember leaving the meeting with second thoughts. Both of us did. We said, "Let's think about it and get back to each other in 24 hours."

We would be getting Curt Flood and Joe Taylor, an outfielder, from the Reds. We were giving up Marty Kutyna and Ted Wieand, two right-handed pitchers with pretty good arms, and a minor-leaguer. Fred Hutchinson was our manager in St. Louis then. I remember, as an afterthought to the meeting, saying to Hutchinson, "These guys we're getting are unproven." The pitchers we were giving up were, too.

I certainly had some fear and trepidation. This was my first big-league deal. It wasn't a blockbuster by any means. But it was one thing to watch Frank Lane making all kinds of trades for two years. Now it was me doing it. Darn right, it's different!

Hutchinson said, "Awww, come on. I've heard about Curt Flood and his ability."

Flood was a third baseman then. He'd been up with the Reds for five games in '56 and and three games in '57, all at third base. We didn't need a third baseman because we had Ken Boyer.

But Hutchinson said, "Flood can run and throw. He could probably play the outfield. Let's don't worry about it."

Hutch was kind of the final touch for me, to give me some confidence. So on December 5, 1957, I made my first deal.

Curt Flood was just a kid. He didn't turn 20 until the next month. But in 1958 he played 121 games for us, one at third base and 120 in the outfield. He hit .261 that first year and had 18 assists.

I didn't know that Curt Flood would be our center fielder for 12 years and play in three World Series for the Cardinals. Again, it wasn't my thinking to move him to the outfield. That was Hutch's doing.

From pitching in the big leagues and managing, Hutch had developed a certain attitude. It's the same one that Johnny Keane and Joe McDonald and Whitey Herzog and Bob Kennedy all had. They knew the game. They had opinions. They made decisions. They spoke up.

There's no question about the value of those kinds of people. I admired that and I appreciated that. And my philosophy about trades started right there: Get opinions from the people you trust. Make the deal. Hope you get lucky.

I was so lucky that my first deal was successful. And I always had a special feeling for Curt Flood.

Erasing the Color Line

Tom Alston was the first black player the Cardinals ever signed.

When Fred Saigh owned the club, they wouldn't sign blacks. So they missed the top black prospect from St. Louis, Elston Howard. He was a catcher, and the Yankees signed him. Howard was the Most Valuable Player in the American League in '63 and wound up playing in the World Series 10 times, the last time with Boston in '68.

But then Anheuser-Busch bought the Cardinals in '53. And in 1954, the club purchased Tom Alston from San Diego in the Pacific Coast League for $100,000. I had nothing to do with that signing. But after the Cardinals signed him in 1954, they sent him to Rochester in Triple A, where I was then the general manager.

Tom Alston was a first baseman. He was a good Triple A ballplayer but kind of an average big-league prospect. He played 79 games for us in Rochester in '54 and hit .297 with seven homers, five triples and 15 doubles.

He had a certain amount of pressure on him, let's face it. He was supposed to be, and was, the direction that Major League Baseball was going. And the direction the Cardinals were going. Which was about time.

But for years after Jackie Robinson broke the color line in baseball, spring training in Florida was still segregated. The black ballplayers had to shop around and find families to stay with at spring training. When Mr. Rickey was the general manager years before, his chauffeur had to find somewhere else to stay in Florida. I remember the chauffeur telling me that they drove up to the team's hotel and Mr. Rickey told him, "I'm staying here. You find your own place."

When Mr. Busch bought the ball club in '53, he had some close acquaintances of his buy a hotel in St. Petersburg. Norman Probstein, who had a hotel background in St. Louis, and Morton May, who owned Famous-Barr, made the purchase.

Actually, there were two hotels adjacent to each other in St. Petersburg, right near a causeway. You could walk across from one to the other. They bought them so that they could incorporate the two hotels. They used the smaller one for the ballplayers, black and white, and the larger one for the public.

That's how we integrated it, and that broke the ice. After that, things moved pretty quickly down there.

This whole move was orchestrated by Mr. Busch. Not directly, but by his desire to make this change. He made up his mind to do it. And Al Fleishman, with his PR background, was in the mix and supported it.

Really, the time had come.

What's the Fuss?

For me, personally, it just wasn't an issue to have blacks in baseball. And it never should have been.

I never really understood segregation. Number one, I was not brought up that way. Number two, I spent so much time playing in the parks around St. Louis with all kinds of kids that it never hit me that race should be an issue. I was playing against black basketball players all the time.

Back in the '30s in St. Louis, that was unusual and—to many white people—frightening. But I hadn't looked at it like that before I started playing with black kids, and I didn't afterward, either.

There was never any trouble at those games. It was just a bunch of guys playing basketball. And it only firmed up my opinion that those players weren't any different from me.

I used to get kidded by people when I graduated from college. They said, "Your name must be Levine, not Devine."

The reason was that I was playing basketball with all the Jewish guys. That's when I played my best basketball.

I was in the class of '38 at Washington U. Then I played for the next two years with the YMHA, the Young Men's Hebrew Association. It was similar to the YMCA, the Young Men's Christian Association. The YMHA had one of the best semipro teams in St. Louis. The best guys on the team were Dave Goldberg and Moeie Geeser. The coach was Harry Reget.   I played with them until I left town in '41 for Johnson City to work as the business manager for the Cardinals' Class D team.

We were playing games around St. Louis, and one time we had a game in a city gym against an all-black team. These were separate teams—segregated. And I remember somebody I knew making an issue of that: "You better watch out, these are tough guys."

Playing against this black team, it suddenly hit you: "These guys are just like you. What's the difference but in the color?"

That was my first memorable experience with race. And it never registered as an issue with me. We just had a basketball game with those guys, and it was kind of an indelible feeling that there was no difference. We were all the same. Color didn't make a difference.

Naturally Colorblind

As I said, race was never an issue for me as a fan growing up. As a fan, it wouldn't have bothered me a bit to bring in a ballplayer like Jackie Robinson who could help teams win.

When I became a general manager with the Cardinals in '57, I was just looking for ballplayers, not looking for a specific skin color. Black or white, it didn't make any difference to me. When I made the trades for Curt Flood and Lou Brock, white guys went out and black guys came in. I don't remember any criticism or complaints locally about color, either.

All you had to have was the courage to do it for baseball reasons. Actually, I never received any hate mail for racial reasons. Or if I did, it was so insignificant that it didn't stick in my memory.

But this was not a crusade. I was just doing my job. I wasn't trying to change the way of the world, just trying to change the ball club and win a pennant.

The Beer Baron
and the Teetotaler

My mother and father never drank or smoked. My father lived to be 75 years old, and my mother lived to 105. And I have never drunk alcohol or smoked in my life.

Early in my career with the Cardinals, when I came back to St. Louis as assistant general manager in the '50s, I became known as a Coca-Cola drinker. We'd have a meeting up at the executive dining room at Anheuser-Busch, and I would order a Coke. The first time I did that, someone said, "You better not order a Coke up here in the brewery's dining room. Mr. Busch won't like it."

But when Mr. Busch found out, he never tried to get me to drink beer. We'd be out somewhere, and he'd order a round of Budweisers for everyone. Then he'd always say, "And bring one Coke!"

Hutch Out, Solly In

When I took over as Cardinals general manager after the season in '57, Fred Hutchinson was the manager. He'd been there for two years while I was the assistant to Frank Lane. I liked Fred Hutchinson, even though I had nothing to do with hir-

"The Little Binger:" That's me circa 1920, at about age four, in our house in the St. Louis suburb of Overland. *(Courtesy of Bing Devine)*

Kitchen Cabinet: They didn't like all of my trades, but (left to right) Jane, Joanne, Janice and Mary knew where their bread was buttered! *(Courtesy of Bing Devine)*

Mr. Busch: Cardinals owner August A. Busch Jr., left, made me the first GM ever hired, fired, rehired—and fired again!—by the same team. *(Courtesy of Bing Devine)*

Hoop It Up: Basketball was my best sport, as Solly Hemus, left, found out in his short term as Cardinals manager. *(Courtesy of Bing Devine)*

The Graduate: If someone calls me Vaughan, they must have known me at University City High, where I was Class of '33.

(Courtesy of Bing Devine)

Best Steal: When we acquired Lou Brock, right, from the Cubs, I had no idea he would hit and run his way into the Hall of Fame. *(Courtesy of Bing Devine)*

Trader Lane: I learned to be aggressive in my apprenticeship during '55 and '56 with Cards GM Frank Lane, shown here with me at spring training. *(Courtesy of Bing Devine)*

Let's Go Mets: I had too much respect for Mets president and GM George Weiss, left, to work behind his back when I came on board as a "special assistant." *(AP/WWP)*

Worst Trade: I did everything I could to keep from trading Steve Carlton, but I'd have followed him out of town if I hadn't made the deal. *(AP/WWP)*

Triple A: That's me with manager Harry "The Hat" Walker, left, and coach Lou Kahn when I was GM of the Rochester Red Wings in '54. *(AP/WWP)*

Vietnam Blues: That's me to the right of Martha Raye, center, the fearless entertainer on our USO Tour of Vietnam. Comedian Joey Bishop is at the far left. *(Courtesy of Bing Devine)*

GM at Work: A good GM must be able to read the paper and dictate at the same time…and be able to count on great assistants like Judy Carpenter Barada, right. *(Courtesy of Bing Devine)*

Gracious Lady: Mrs. Joan Payson, shown here greeting a Vietnam War hero, hired me a month after the Cardinals fired me in '64 and was a wonderful owner. *(Courtesy of Bing Devine)*

Mr. Rickey: Little did I know that when Branch Rickey returned to spring training with the Cardinals, here in '63, I'd be fired 18 months later. *(AP/WWP)*

Best Deal: In Johnson City, I traded the player who was dating Mary Anderson. She then agreed to marry me after that '41 season…and hasn't fired me yet! *(Courtesy of Bing Devine)*

The Man: Stan Musial, right, one of the all-time great players and gentlemen, has been a wonderful friend for almost 50 years. *(Courtesy of Bing Devine)*

GM Material: Four general managers—Lee Thomas (far left), myself, Walt Jocketty (second from right) and Dal Maxvill (far right)—and one who should have been—Mike Shannon (center), my favorite overachiever. *(Courtesy of Bing Devine)*

New Skippers: After the upheaval of '64, Red Schoendienst, left, went to spring training the next year as the new manager in St. Louis, and Johnny Keane, right, ended up with the Yankees. *(AP/WWP)*

Movin' On Up: Mary boxes up the girls—Joanne on the left, Janice in the middle and six-month-old Jane—for our move from Rochester to St. Louis in '55. *(Courtesy of Bing Devine)*

The Miracle Men: I signed Gil Hodges, right, to manage the Mets during the '67 World Series, but I returned to St. Louis before he ever went to work for me. *(Courtesy of Bing Devine)*

Beginner's Luck? Curt Flood, shown here seven years after he came to St. Louis in '58, turned my first trade into a winner. *(AP/WWP)*

ing him, and I got to know him pretty well. So he managed for me again in '58, but I didn't even have him for one full year.

After 144 games, we were 69 and 75 and in fifth place. That's when we replaced Hutchinson. Stan Hack finished the year and went 3-7, and we wound up in sixth place out of eight teams in the National League. We were a game ahead of Los Angeles and three games ahead of Philadelphia. And we were 20 games behind Milwaukee, who won the pennant.

But I didn't fire Hutch. Here's what happened. Late in the season, Dick Meyer, whose name creeps into a lot of stories from those days, called me and said:

"We need to talk about the team, what we need to do and how we need to do it. I want you to develop a report on the Cardinals club, the whole situation. Then I want you to bring it to a meeting that I'll set up with you, me and Mr. Busch at his place out at Grant's Farm."

So I wrote my report, and I spent a lot of time on it. Remember, this was really my first opportunity to be a general manager.

When we had our meeting, I handed the report to Mr. Busch. It featured rehiring Fred Hutchinson, changing coaches, and a lot of my opinions on our personnel—where we were strong, where we were weak, and what we had hoped to do.

Mr. Busch took the report and put it on his desk. He didn't read it. He didn't even open it.

Then he said to Dick, "Well, are you going to tell him, or should I?"

Dick said, "Well, this is your idea, so why don't you tell him."

So Mr. Busch said, "Well, we're going to get rid of Fred Hutchinson. And you don't need to think about replacing him, because I already have the manager—Solly Hemus."

Solly was an infielder we had traded to Philadelphia in '56. He had been with the Cardinals since '49, and when he left here he wrote Mr. Busch a note. Al Fleishman, Mr. Busch's publicist, told me about it. And in the note, Solly said something like:

"I really enjoyed playing with the Cardinals. I want to congratulate you on having a wonderful organization. If there's ever any reason to bring me back, I'd appreciate it, because I love the Cardinals and St. Louis."

This made a great impression on Mr. Busch. And I can understand that.

Solly Hemus was a gung-ho player. He really hustled. He got more out of his ability than he should have. And all of that impressed Mr. Busch, along with the letter that Solly wrote when he left.

So Dick Meyer got the handoff from Mr. Busch and told me, "I've already paved the way for you to talk to the Phillies. It's up to you to make a suitable arrangement with John Quinn."

Quinn was the general manager in Philadelphia. He was the father of Jack Quinn, who later was president of the St. Louis Blues hockey team.

So on September 29, 1958, I acquired second baseman Solly Hemus from Philadelphia for Gene Freese, a third baseman. But we really traded for a manager.

Rolling with the Punches

Yes, I was kind of hurt by the whole process of firing Hutchinson and hiring Hemus. I was kind of young. I had just really become a general manager the year before. I had made what I thought was a thorough report, and the determination was made for me without my views being considered.

But as a general manager, you're not going to have the final say. Frank Lane found that out when he tried to trade Musial. He had to clear his trades with someone above him. He wasn't used to that, that slowed him down, and so he left. I think I had already realized that this is business. Sooner or later, somewhere along the line, everybody has somebody ahead of him.

So I sat down with Solly and worked out a contract for him to be our field manager. He was only 35 and he still wanted to play. He actually did play 24 games in '59.

Even though he wasn't my choice, I liked him. That may sound strange, but you've got to know Solly Hemus. He was a hell-bent-for-leather player. Yeah, he was young, but managing didn't scare him. His personality when he took over was, "Come on, boys, let's go! I'm ready!"

The thing with Solly was that he really didn't think he needed any advice. He was sure he knew what he wanted to do. We all run into that problem when we're over-simplifying things, and Solly had a tendency to do that as a manager. He found out that it wasn't as simple as he thought it was. And it didn't work out the way Mr. Busch wanted it to.

Solly only managed for two and a half years. But he went on to a lot of success in his life. He made a lot of money in the oil business in Texas. He's in Houston, and I still talk to him on the phone occasionally. When things didn't work out with Hemus, I replaced him midway through the '61 season with Keane. It only took three years for Johnny Keane to win the pennant and the World Series. And for me to get fired. And for him to leave.

Harder Than It Looks

After Johnny Keane became my manager in the early '60s, Gabe Paul and I again talked at the winter meetings.

Gabe called me in the hotel, saying, "Why can't we make a deal? I haven't made a deal in a long time."

I said, "Me neither."

So we tried to come up with something, having made deals together before. But we couldn't come up with anything.

So Gabe said, "Hey, let's let the managers see if they can make one."

Hutchinson was managing the Reds then. So Gabe talked to him and I talked to Keane, and they said okay. After they talked, Keane said to me, "Hutch and I have made a deal."

Of course it was subject to the approval of the general managers.

I called Gabe and he said that Hutch had told him about this deal. And then Gabe said, "It's so bad I can't announce it. If that's the only deal I make at the meetings, it's worse than not making any deal!"

I said, "I agree with you. Let's forget it!"

Everybody thinks it's so easy to make a trade. Here Gabe and I couldn't get one done, and then we hoped the managers could make a deal of some substance and they couldn't do it either.

Now another factor enters into it for general managers today—the budgetary factor. Because of the huge contracts the players have, it's an even greater difficulty.

I can't tell you much about that deal that Keane and Hutch wanted to make. I do know it was one-for-one, but the players were so insignificant I can't even remember who they were. All I remember is you wondered why you had the one, much less why you would want to acquire the other one.

Bill White, Future President

Our first baseman in '64 was Bill White. I had traded Sam Jones for him, and that wasn't a very popular deal, either.

That's understandable, really. People didn't know about the player you were getting when you gave up someone they liked. And you heard about it pretty quickly.

I made that trade in spring training of '59. When I got the recommendation from Eddie Stanky, our scouting director, I was at a phone booth on the beach in St. Petersburg. We didn't have cell phones then, and it was a phone booth or nothing. But that's how you did it if you weren't at the office. You'd drive up and down the beach till you found a pay phone.

Stanky was out west watching the Giants. I remember picking Stanky's brain, asking him, "How well do you like him?"

Stanky said, "Let's not debate it. You sent me out here to see him. I like him. I'm telling you right now, I'd make the deal. And I suggest you do, too!"

You've got to realize that when you're scouting and getting an opinion, everyone else has one, too. But some people, if you talk to them long enough, they'll take a position that isn't solid but wavering, not saying yes or no.

Stanky wasn't like that. He was an A, B, C, D guy. He would tell you what he thought. That's what I liked about him.

So we made the deal, and Stanky was right. White turned out better than we had reason to hope. He was 25 years old then. He had only played two years with the Giants and was barely a .250 hitter. He was in St. Louis for six years and hit better than .300, or close to it, every year. And he was good at first base, too.

I can't say I knew that Bill White would go on to become president of the National League. But it didn't surprise me. I recognized right away that Bill had that real ability not to let anybody talk him down or out of what he thought. He's still a strong-minded guy, that's one thing I'll say about him. He's not going to waffle on anything. And that's the way he was 45 years ago when we first acquired him.

I never had any kind of special relationship with him. It's not like I did anything that helped him become a baseball executive. The guy who became close to Bill White was Harry Walker. In the off season, Bill would go down to Alabama and go fishing with Harry. Bill was black and Harry was a southern white, but they didn't care about that. That's the kind of guys they were.

Getting Julian Javier

We acquired Julian Javier from Pittsburgh for Wilmer Mizell, a left-handed pitcher. And Javier was really a project when he arrived. But that was Stanky, too. He was really high on Javier. We made the trade in May of '60, and it really did help both teams.

Mizell helped the Pirates win the pennant and the World Series that year. Javier started at second base for us for the next 12 years and played in three World Series. He became a great second baseman and a leader on the team. Javier didn't say much, but in his quiet way he was a strong individual.

We had a lot of leaders on that '64 team: Bill White, Ken Boyer, Julian Javier and Dick Groat. And there couldn't have been anybody more strong-minded than Curt Flood, with what he did later to test baseball's reserve clause.

Those kinds of players strengthened everyone around them.

HE NEVER SPEAKS A BAD WORD ABOUT ANYONE

STAN MUSIAL REFLECTS ON BING DEVINE

Bing's been in baseball a lot of years, and he loves the game. He loves baseball and the Cardinals, and he worked his way up and got to be the general manager.

Bing is an easy-going guy, and he listens. Bing was always a good listener.

I had contract dealings with Bing, and we never had any problems. He always treated me very fairly. In fact, one year, about 1957 or so, I saw that Ralph Kiner, with the Pirates, got a contract for $90,000. I was talking to Bing, and I said, "I think I should be the highest-paid player in the National League. I want $91,000."

I went on a trip and came back, and Bing called me in to talk about my contract. I asked him, "Did I get the $91,000?"

And he said, "No!"

Then he said, "Mr. Busch wants you to be the first $100,000 player."

Bing was always a good baseball man. He made some of the greatest trades the Cardinals ever made. He brought Brock, Flood, White, Javier, Groat…the guys who won the World Series in '64.

And Bing put that '67 club together that won the World Series. He was with the Mets then, but that was his club in '67, even though I was the general manager. Red was the manager and we had a young veteran club. All of them had six or seven years in the big leagues.

But we didn't make many trades after Bing left. Red and I didn't have to make many moves. We brought a young pitcher up from the minors, Jack Lamabe I think. And we got Roger Maris in '67 from the Yankees. His salary was $75,000, which surprised me. I thought it would be more, with him being from New York and considering all that he'd accomplished as a player there.

But after that one year as general manager, I decided to step down. I couldn't look after the Cardinals and look after my properties. I had the restaurant and the bowling alley here in St. Louis and three hotels—one in Miami Beach, one in Clearwater and the Airport Hilton here.

I couldn't do both, look after my enterprises and the ball club. And my enterprises were doing much better than what I was making in baseball!

So when I decided to step down as general manager, Dick Meyer and I brought Bing's name up. Bing was a good, solid baseball man. And I think the Cardinals wanted to do a favor, to bring Bing back because of what happened to him in '64.

When they let him go the first time, I don't know what they were thinking. I know Dick Meyer didn't want to let Bing go, but Branch Rickey undermined him. Busch realized he made a mistake.

I didn't know that Bing kept Rickey from getting me to retire a year earlier than I did. But that's Bing: He takes a stand and he sticks with it.

We've been friends all these years and I see him often. His wife Mary and my wife Lil were the best of friends all these years. We know the family very well. He's one of my best friends, no question about it.

And one thing about Bing is that he never says anything negative about anybody.

Chapter 7

Going Home Again

The Reunion

My career wasn't all mapped out evenly, that's for sure. In December of '67, when I came back to the Cards the second time as general manager, it was the first time I was not chasing someone's shadow. When I was the Cardinals' GM the first time, Branch Rickey was also with the Cardinals, and I had to work out that tricky relationship. And when I was the GM in New York, I had to work out my relationship with George Weiss.

Not only did I have to put together a club in both places, I had to assert my authority because of the situation I was in. I didn't have to do that when I came back to the Cardinals from '68 to '78. We did go back to the World Series in '68. I just wish we had had a better ball club as we moved on.

But when I came back in December of '67, the Cards had just won the World Series. Obviously I had no building to do. But that was okay. I never felt like I had to make a deal just to make one. I never was that way, like Frank Lane was.

I did make a trade in February of '68 to get a pretty good catcher named Johnny Edwards from Cincinnati. He came in to back up Tim McCarver. During the season, I also got Pete Mikkelsen, a pitcher from the Cubs, and Ron Davis, an outfielder from Houston.

But to be honest, I'd done most of the building on that team before I was fired in '64. I had traded for Lou Brock in left field, Curt Ford in center field and Julian Javier at second base. McCarver, Mike Shannon at third and Dal Maxvill at short were all in our farm system when I left. The only regulars I didn't have anything to do with were Orlando Cepeda at first base and Roger Maris in right field—two key players.

Look at our pitching staff. They got Joe Hoerner from Houston in '66. But Bob Gibson, Nelson Briles, Steve Carlton, Ray Washburn, Larry Jaster and Wayne Granger were all in the system when I left in '64.

I guess you could say that I didn't have to build that '68 team because I already had.

Going Four for Six

I hadn't really thought about it till somebody just brought it up. But from 1964 to 1969, I helped build four of the six National League teams that went to the World Series—the Cardinals in '64, '67 and '68, and the Mets in '69. Three of them wound up winning the World Series. The only one that lost was the '68 Cardinals, and that's the only one in which I was still the general manager during the World Series. So I never got to hoist a World Series trophy in the locker room.

I didn't go to many, if any, of the World Series games in '64 after I'd just been fired by the Cardinals. It would've been too hard. I can't remember my emotions except to use that word I've used so often: bittersweet. I don't remember it, but I have a newspaper article that says I went into the Cardinals' locker room to congratulate everyone after we won. It still felt like "we," even though I'd already been hired by the Mets that September.

When I was with the Mets, I don't think I went to all the games when the Cardinals were in the '67 World Series. I did interview Gil Hodges at one game in St. Louis about our managing job. When the series moved to Boston, I went back through New York and stopped over and went to the office. I went up to Boston, where we made the announcement in the hotel about signing Hodges. I didn't go to any of the games there. I just did my business and left.

It wasn't that painful to see the Cardinals in the series at that point. I'd mellowed about that. I had my own problems with the Mets, and I was busy working on them.

Obviously, I went to all the World Series games in '68 when I was back with the Cardinals as general manager. But I didn't think about any kind of vindication or anything of that nature. It was kind of ancient history, even though it was still pretty much the same team that I'd left in '64, except for Cepeda and Maris. I had something else to concentrate on. We were trying to beat Detroit for the world championship. That's all I was thinking about then.

The misplayed fly ball in center field by Curt Flood in Game 7 is the only thing I can remember about that series. I can picture that moment and what a key factor it was. It probably cost us the ballgame and the series. And it was so strange because Flood was such a great center fielder. You'd never expect him to misplay a ball like that. And in his own ballpark.

When the Mets won the World Series in '69, I don't remember going to any games. I had something else to do then in St. Louis. My attitude wasn't: "Look what you did back then." It became more important to say: "What are you going to do now?"

Just the satisfaction of having a hand in the success is enough. I don't need a trophy. My thinking was, and is, the same process that I applied to making deals: Make the decision. Hope you get lucky. And go on to your next decision.

The Redhead

Red Schoendienst was the manager when I came back to St. Louis. And he was unbelievable, as he'd been as a player.

Red was never one for emotion, one way or another, as a player. When I first knew him, before Frank Lane traded him away in '56, he was a producer. He didn't have a lot of flair about him, but he got the job done. And he still does. He's 80, and he still hits fungos to the Cardinal infielders during batting practice. Then he goes up to the press box with Walt Jocketty, the general manager, and calmly watches and analyzes the game.

Stan Musial was a great player, but he was also a great businessman. And he is still a great businessman, with his Stan the Man, Inc. Red's had some business ventures, too, but nothing like Stan. Baseball was Red's life, when you come right down to it. He's stayed in a big-league uniform for 60 years.

Did Stan have flair when he played? Sure he did. But Red wasn't like that. I'm not demeaning Schoendienst, but the two had different styles. And Red had to go through his problem with tuberculosis, which was really serious when he had it as a young player. He couldn't be with his family. It's a contagious disease, and he had to be quarantined. His family had to come down and talk to him through a window at the hospital.

That was almost 50 years ago, and he's still going strong.

Gibson the Competitor

I was a new general manager in '57 when we talked to our scout, who had a great interest in a young pitcher from Omaha named Bob Gibson. I wasn't involved personally in scouting Gibson. But I remember hearing this scout—and I can't remember exactly who it was—talking about him. The story surfaced that Gibson was a basketball player and a Globetrotter. But he was definitely a baseball prospect.

You can point to Gibson as the model of a great competitor. You talk about someone who fought the opposition on a ballfield! I remember walking through our clubhouse once before a game, and Gibson was talking to some of his teammates.

He told them, "I saw two of you guys talking to the opposition before the game today, socializing with them. I'm not pitching today, so you do what you want.

"But I just want you to know that when I'm pitching, don't be talking to the other team. Because that's the enemy. And I better not catch you talking to the enemy before I go out to pitch."

I think the modern pitcher who's most like Gibson in terms of mindset while pitching a game is Woody Williams with the Cardinals. Williams is a competitor. And he can pitch and hit, for that matter, just like Gibson could hit. Tony La Russa lets Williams bat for himself late in a game with runners on base, the same thing Gibson's managers did with him.

The thing about Gibson is that when you look back, it's hard to pick out his best games. You kind of lump all of his games together. There aren't any highs and lows. They're all highs.

Hiring Joe Medwick

Before the 1969 season, I hired Joe Medwick as a minor league batting instructor...even though he was a little rough on me when I couldn't fight back. I was just a kid in the publicity office 30 years before when I was pitching batting practice to him, and I was almost proud that Medwick took a shot at me in the clubhouse. It was like a medal of valor. I wasn't close enough to Medwick back then for him to even notice me, really, but I think he knew that he was my hero.

I described myself as inclined to be shy when I was a kid. My father would influence me to try to get autographs at the ballpark, and I wouldn't do it. I didn't want to get turned down.

So after I came back to the Cardinals a second time as general manager, we had a need for a minor league batting instructor.

Somebody said, "You ought to consider Medwick."

My first thought was, "It makes sense."

The name made sense. The background made sense. Thinking back to the kind of ballplayer he was and the hero he was to me as a fan—it made sense. He was on the level of Mark McGwire, a big strong hitter.

And I thought Medwick did a good job for us.

Vietnam Tour

After the '68 World Series, my first year back as general manager, I went to Vietnam on a USO tour. I received the invitation, and I called Stan Musial. I knew he went the year before. I asked Stan if he had any advice, and he said, "Don't go!"

And it was rough. It was a heck of a lot rougher and more dangerous than the three years I spent in the Pacific during World War II, when I was stationed the whole time in Hawaii. I was in the navy from late 1943 to mid-1945. I missed the '44 World Series here between the Cardinals and the Browns, but I listened to it on Armed Forces Radio.

The navy sent me to communications school and then to Kaneohe Bay, Hawaii. I was with the Navy Fleet Air Wing 2. We handled the radio traffic coming in from the West Coast and out to the front, and we broke codes.

How rough was that, being in Hawaii? I never got anywhere near the fighting. The only hard part was being away from Mary. We had an 11-month-old baby, Joanne, when I went in.

When I went to Vietnam, there were six of us from Major League Baseball. I was with Ron Swoboda, the outfielder I'd had with the Mets, and Larry Jackson, a pitcher with the Phillies. Al Fleishman, who handled public relations for Gussie Busch and the Cardinals, was with Ernie Banks of the Cubs and a pitcher named Pete Richert from the Dodgers.

We flew into Saigon to start the tour, and they were taking fire at the airport. So the pilot had to fly back and forth until it was finally safe enough to land.

I thought, "Uh-oh, that's a great start. Musial was right!"

My group went south and worked our way up. Al's group went north and worked their way down. Then we met up at Saigon to come home.

One time, we were in a whaleboat going up this canal. Every time we came to a hut along the bank, someone had to raise the fishing nets that the people in the hut used. Otherwise we couldn't get through.

And every time this happened, the enlisted man running the boat would say, "We're set up for an ambush."

So they gave me a grenade launcher.

I said, "I don't know how to shoot a gun."

They said, "You might need it."

And I said, "If I need it, we're hopeless!"

The same thing would happen when we went out in a Jeep. We'd be going along and the driver would say, "We've got to stop here. They're taking fire up ahead."

We never got shot at, but we were in danger. At least that's what they'd tell us. I don't know if they were putting us on or not.

We were there for 17 days. When we got to a base, we would talk to the troops and take questions. They were most interested in asking about clubs, players, pennant races. I'm sure if you went anywhere now the troops would have the same kinds of questions. But it was eye-opening for me, being exposed to that kind of danger.

Martha Raye, the entertainer, was also on that tour. She wasn't with us every day. Occasionally we'd go to an advance base together and she'd go up in the helicopter with us. One time, a helicopter was taking us someplace. We got word that it was unsafe to land because they were taking fire down there. The pilot said he was turning around and going back.

Martha said, "Well, I'm a colonel"—she'd been over there so much that they had made her an honorary colonel—"and I'm telling you we're going in!"

And we did.

But I was sitting there thinking, "Hey, Martha, leave him alone!"

Taking Heat for Torre

After we lost to Detroit in the '68 World Series, I made a couple of deals that same October that I liked.

In one deal, we got Houston reliever Dave Giusti for Johnny Edwards. And I made a deal with Cincinnati for Vada Pinson, an outfielder who could really run, in exchange for Wayne Granger and Bobby Tolan. Pinson was to replace the production provided by Roger Maris, who retired after the '68 season.

But I made the big deal a year later in spring training on March 17, 1969: Orlando Cepeda to Atlanta for Joe Torre. And nobody liked it.

The two deals that I made that were most controversial—and that nobody could see the reasons for—were Brock and Torre. I turned out to be right on both of them. But you don't gloat. When you make deals, you know you're going to be wrong on occasion if you make enough of them.

Broglio was popular in St. Louis when we traded him for Brock, but Cepeda was a lot more popular with Cardinals fans when we traded him for Torre. Cepeda was the National League's Most Valuable Player in '67. He led the Cards to the world championship in '67 and back to the World Series in '68. And then the next spring, I traded him away. Cepeda was three years older than Torre, and I thought Cepeda might be on the way down.

Cepeda for Torrre really was not a bad deal, when it was all said and done. And neither was acquiring Pinson to replace Maris, if you look at what both of them accomplished their first year in St. Louis compared to what Cepeda and Maris did the year before. In '68, Cepeda hit .248 with 16 homers and 73 runs batted in. In '69, Torre hit .289 with 18 homers and 101 RBIs. In '68, Maris hit .255 with five homers and 45 RBIs. In '69, Pinson also hit .255 but with 10 homers and 70 RBIs.

Torre had been a first baseman in Atlanta after starting out as a catcher. When we got him, we thought we could move him to third base. We didn't do it right away, though. The first year, he played almost all of the time at first base. The next year, he played first base and caught. But the third year, he played 161 games at third base. The second year he was in St. Louis, he hit .321. The third year, 1971, he hit .363 and collected 230 hits and 137 runs batted in and led the league in all three categories.

Torre had six very good years in St. Louis before I sent him to the Mets. He was one of my favorite deals on the basis of his long-term success.

Torre's success was not only as a player, but also as a manager. It didn't work out when he was managing the Cardinals in the '90s, but it certainly worked out after that when he went to the Yankees. He became one of the great managers of all time.

Trading Steve Carlton

As a young pitcher, Steve Carlton was difficult to sign. He wasn't a holdout, but as a young player he was always a problem at contract time.

Carlton had a high opinion of himself. Rightly so, as it turned out. But Mr. Busch didn't like that. Here was a young pitcher who hadn't established himself. And Mr. Busch heard, without the specific details, that this young pitcher was always difficult to sign.

In 1970, Carlton led the league with 19 losses. His career record at that point was 57 wins, 53 losses. He turned around the next year and went 20-9. But his earned run average was 3.56, and he only had 172 strikeouts in 273 innings.

I'd like to think that I could have kept Carlton around to see how great he would become. All I knew at the time was that he was a good young left-handed pitcher who had just turned 27, and I thought we should keep him. But his contract was up again that off season. Mr. Busch had a meeting with me and Dick Meyer, his right-hand man at Anheuser-Busch. And the team brain trust, if that's what you want to call it, decided that we ought to trade Carlton because we didn't have him signed and he wanted too much money.

Basically, Mr. Busch wanted him gone.

His attitude was, "Who does that young whippersnapper think he is, telling us what to do? He hasn't done that much to this point."

Carlton was a strong personality in his own right. He wasn't intimidated by Gussie Busch, and that contributed to it. We were dealing in different times then, too. The big salaries weren't here yet.

So I started calling other teams to determine what the interest was in Carlton. And every day, Dick Meyer would call me and ask if I'd received any offers.

One day, he called and said, "Mr. Busch comes through my office every morning at the brewery and asks me, 'Has Devine traded Carlton yet?' So please trade him soon, because my ulcer's acting up worse every day."

That was his way of putting some humor into something serious, of throwing a little light comment into something that was the hard truth. Dick Meyer was the best ever at handling a crisis like that.

Finally, one day he called and said, "Is there anything new on trading Carlton?"

I said, "There's some interest from John Quinn with the Phillies."

Dick said, "For whom?"

I said, "For Rick Wise."

Dick hung up. He called back a little later and said, "Can you make that deal within 24 hours?"

I said, "That might be pushing it. I can't guarantee that, but I'll try to make it as soon as I can."

Dick said, "Well, make it within 48 hours, for the sake of my ulcer."

So I got back with John Quinn, the Phillies general manager, and we traded Carlton for Wise on February 25, 1972.

People forget now, but Rick Wise was a pretty good pitcher then. He was 17-14 the year before but his earned run average was

2.88, much better than Carlton's ERA in '71. And Wise had 155 strikeouts in 272 innings, almost as many as Carlton had in '71.

The fans and media didn't like the deal, but they did not have that realization yet of how great Carlton would become. Of course, Carlton went on to greatness, starting with his first year in Philly. He went 27-10 and led the league in wins, earned run average, strikeouts and innings pitched. By the time his career was finished, he had won over 300 games and made the Hall of Fame as one of the greatest left-handers of all time.

Wise went 16-16 his first year in St. Louis and 16-12 the next year, and then we shipped him to Boston.

I don't want to cop a plea here, but getting rid of Carlton was not a deal that I initiated or tried to talk anybody into. It was just the relationship between Carlton and Mr. Busch, who said, "Let's get rid of him." That meant he had to go, so Dick Meyer said, "Let's get it over with."

I dragged my feet as long as I could, because I didn't want to do it. I don't like to second-guess my deals, but after that one I did wonder: What if I had made a stronger effort to change Mr. Busch's mind?

So I asked Dick what would have happened if I hadn't moved Carlton within those 48 hours.

Dick laughed and said, "I'll tell you what would have happened. You'd have been gone first…and Carlton would have been gone right after you."

And that answered my question!

The Rearview Mirror

I look back—and I know it's second-guessing—but I wonder what could have happened if we kept Carlton? People have analyzed and enumerated the number of pennants we would have won with him. And I can't argue with them. I think we would have won a couple pennants in the '70s with Carlton. At least we certainly would have had a better chance than we did without him.

Carlton and I used to see each other in St. Louis, because he continued to live here for years. He was always friendly. He never seemed mad. And when you think of it, he couldn't have been mad at me. The trade worked to his advantage.

He could never say, "What could I have done if I had stayed in St. Louis?"

How could he have done any better than what he did in Philly?

WORKING 48 HOURS A DAY

RED SCHOENDIENST REFLECTS ON BING DEVINE

In 1964, we were in Houston at old Colt .45 Stadium. It was hotter than hell. I mean hot. There was no air conditioning, and the fans didn't help a bit because the humidity was so high up there.

I was a coach then, and Bing and Johnny Keane called me into the office in the locker room. They started asking me what I thought about Lou Brock.

I said, "Oh, can you get him?"

They just said, "What do you think about Brock?"

I said, "I really haven't seen him that much. He's strong, the way he looks. I've watched him in batting practice and he hits the ball hard. He's got a good arm, but I don't know how accurate it is. And you know he can run."

They kept talking about him, and I said, "Can you get him?"

They said, "Well, yeah."

I said, "Who you gonna give up?"

They said, "Never mind! We're just asking questions."

Then somebody, I can't remember if it was Johnny or Bing, said, "Well, he's not a good outfielder, is he?"

I said, "Listen, he's playing in Chicago. When I broke in in the '40s, Bill Nicholson was supposed to be a real good outfielder, and he had trouble at Wrigley. Right field is so hard to play there with that sun and that wind."

See, Brock played right field then.

Bing and Johnny kept asking me this and that. Then I left, and both of them called the rest of the coaches in. Vern Benson was there, and he was a good baseball man. I forgot who else was there, but Bing and Johnny asked them all what they thought about Brock.

The next morning, the trade was made. And old Brock, it didn't take him long to make it over to the Cards. Johnny was making up the lineup that night, and he didn't know who to put in there because Brock wasn't in yet. The game was just ready to start, and all of a sudden, here comes Brock…just like an old cornfield player! He was coming in from way down the right field line, which is where the clubhouse was in old Colt Stadium. He had his glove on his bat and his bat on his shoulder. Actually, the glove might have been on his belt. But I remember seeing him walking like that, just real calm, walking all the way in from right field.

When they let Bing go in '64, it didn't look like we had a chance to win. Harry Caray was the announcer then, and he was big for Leo Durocher to come in and manage. I think that's how it all came about when Johnny quit after we won the World Series. He was sick of all the rumors that he was getting fired.

The funny thing is, the year before I was a player-coach. I hit five times as a pinch hitter and went 0 for five. Bing came up to me and said, if I remember it right, that they had to protect some young guys or lose them. The rules were different then.

Bing told me, "There are a number of clubs that would love to have you as a pinch hitter and part-time player, if you want to do that."

I said, "That sounds good."

Then Bing said, "There are some other things we can do with you if you want to stay here."

I said, "Well, tell me about those."

He said, "First, we'll just make you a bench coach but pay you the same salary you're getting now to coach and play…"

I said, "That's all I need to hear. That's good enough for me. I don't want to go anywhere."

And I'm still here. All because Bing gave me that choice, instead of just trading me to get something in return.

Here's the funny thing. The next year, Johnny quit after the World Series, and I ended up the manager. It's crazy, but that's how things happen in baseball. Hey, Bing got fired and we won the World Series a couple of months later with his team.

When Bing was hired by the Mets, I didn't want to see Bing go to New York. As a GM, he was on top of everything all the time. He'd have meetings with Johnny, and the coaches were always invited. He always wanted to get everyone's opinion on things.

Stan was the GM for that one year in '67, when we won it all. He came up to me and said, "This is my last year, Red."

I said, "Why?"

Stan said, "This job is around the clock. I've got other businesses to take care of."

That's when they brought Bing back as GM. And the way he worked at it, it was a 48-hour-a-day job. That's why I never wanted to do it.

I was still the manager when Bing came back after the '67 season. If he saw something he didn't like, he'd question it, but he was great to work for. He always stood back and let the manager do his job.

Chapter 8

Family

The Binger

I had an aunt, my mother's sister, named Daisy. Through her family situation she ended up staying with us for several years when I was young. She's the one who gave me my nickname, Bing. My given name is Vaughan Palmore Devine, but I used to throw things around, and they'd go bing and bang. She'd say, "He's a binger!" Eventually they contracted that to "Bing," and that's what they called me at home.

But when I got to high school, they dropped it. My mother liked the name Vaughan. It was a family name, which is why it's spelled with that second "a," instead of V-a-u-g-h-n. Even now, when somebody will come up to me and say, "Hi, Vaughan," I know that's somebody who knew me from high school. That's what I was known as until I went to college.

When I was at Washington University playing basketball, a writer named Ray Gillespie covered our games. He was with the old *St. Louis Star-Times*. After a while he said to me, "I don't like calling you Vaughan Devine. It doesn't fit right in a headline."

Not that I was in the headlines a lot.

But he said, "Can't you do any better than that?"

I said, "Well, before I got to high school they called me Bing."

Ray started referring to me as "Bing" in his stories, and it's stuck all these years.

A Family Game

What I like is to see families at the ballpark. And to see and hear the senior member of the family update—or downdate—the others about how the game was then and now. It's a game you can talk about and understand from one era to another. It's a family-oriented game, there's no doubt about that. And I guess in our society, that's got to be good.

I became interested in baseball through my father. When I was old enough, not to be driving but to be traveling, we'd take a vacation each summer. We'd drive in our car on a Cardinals road trip. Sometimes it'd be a short one, say to Chicago. A couple times it was an East Coast trip to Pittsburgh, Philadelphia, Boston and New York. We'd miss the first game of a new series, or the last game of the last one, driving to the next city. We made the arrangements on our own but stayed at the same hotel as the ball club.

We're talking about my early teens, which would be the late 1920s or early '30s. My mother, father and I would go. One time I even got to take a friend.

I was an only child. I had a younger sister who died when she was two or three years old. She was born in 1920. I was born in 1916, so I was six or seven years old when it happened. Her name was Barbara Alice, and she died of something you wouldn't die of now. She had scarlet fever and whooping cough. Back then, either one could have killed you.

I remember sitting across the street in the neighbor's yard. It was very somber. She'd had some kind of attack and they couldn't get an emergency vehicle. My dad drove out to Overland and got some medical equipment to bring back from the hospital, probably oxygen, but it was too late.

So I grew up as an only child, and my parents were baseball fans.

The Cardinals won the World Series in 1926 when I was 10, and that was the start of it for me. I think I did see a game in the '26 Series, although I can't remember anything spectacular about it. My dad and I went down and sat in the bleachers. He worked for the Land Title Insurance Company.

A few years later, my dad had box seats with the company. We didn't get to take much advantage of it. The seats would be for the customers. We went to the games occasionally.

Piano Player or Ballplayer?

My mother put me in piano lessons when I was probably about 10 years old. I was at an age when I didn't have any control over what I was going to do. If I had my way, I'd have been doing something else—playing some sport, probably baseball.

I think I ended up taking piano lessons eight to ten years, on into high school. My mother played a little by ear. I think she had a great desire to have her only child exposed to some kind of classical activity. She was a great baseball fan, though. When television came in to fashion, that used to be her favorite program. Baseball...and pro wrestling!

I don't know if I had any musical aptitude. I may have had, but I never really threw myself into it. I did the best I could, but I was never oriented in that direction. I preferred throwing a baseball.

Safe at Home

We lived in Overland, a suburb of St. Louis, until I was 10 years old. There was a vacant lot between our house and the next house up the street. It wasn't a lot you could use as a full-fledged baseball field. It was about the equivalent of a small infield, but you could fantasize and act like Rogers Hornsby.

I'd play an imaginary game by myself. By the hour. I'd take the bat, hit a ball and run the bases. Or throw the ball up and try to catch it. And I'd broadcast what I was doing, just silly stuff like that.

Later on when we moved to University City, right next to the city of St. Louis, I remember doing the same thing with a basketball. We had a basket over the garage. I also did the same thing with a football. I'd throw it up in the air and catch it and avoid tacklers. Sometimes those imaginary tacklers would bring me down. Hey, you have to make it somewhat competitive! There weren't a lot of kids in my neighborhood.

And I'd play step ball, or wall ball. That was great, a real game you could play by yourself between two houses. In step ball, if you hit that edge of the step the ball would fly pretty far. We used to play bottle caps, too. We'd pitch them and hit them. That was at the age of about 15 to 18, and we used to play that in a service station that was lit up at night. One of the guys who played in the game actually served the gasoline. That's back when it was full service, not self service. So when a car came in, he'd have to quit for a minute to take care of the customer.

A Hard Lesson

I was completely engrossed in sports. That's when I really thought I could play professional baseball. In my late teens or early twenties, I went to the Ray Doan Baseball School in Hot Springs, Arkansas. About 500 kids went down there in the spring, all hopeful baseball players, for a four-week session.

Goodness knows how my dad afforded it. And like all parents, let's face it, they wanted me to get my college degree. But I wanted to go, and they sent me.

It was tough. You lived in an old, broken-down hotel. You played on makeshift baseball fields, five or six of them, and they had instruction.

One of the would-be ballplayers was Elmer Dean, a relative of Dizzy and Paul. I don't remember the relationship, but Elmer Dean was one of the group who should have realized they weren't ballplayers.

At that point, I was just playing second base and not trying to pitch. I did get sent over to Pine Bluff, a lower minor league club, for a look. It was a quick look. Then they sent me home.

That Hot Springs baseball school did a lot to me and for me. That's where I ended up playing my best baseball. But that whole experience really sent me back to school. I found out that the life wasn't the greatest, and I got an inkling that maybe I wasn't as good as I thought I was.

I'm not so sure my dad didn't have that in mind. He probably thought, in effect, "Let him get it out of his system."

I went back to school and I got serious my senior year. I could see what was up ahead. And I guess I matured a little bit.

Joanne Goes to Bat for Me

In December of '64, four months after Gussie Busch fired me, Al Fleishman came to me and said, "Joanne wrote a letter to Mr. Busch, and I have it."

Joanne is our oldest daughter. She was going to college at Denison in Ohio, and she thought I'd been treated unfairly. Mr. Busch knew all three of our girls, from spring training and activities at his home at Grant's Farm in St. Louis, and he loved all of them. He thought they were really something special, and of course Mary and I did, too.

We never saw Joanne's letter before she sent it to Mr. Busch. We didn't even know she had written one. But since Al was Mr. Busch's public relations man, the letter wound up with him.

When Al called me, I said, "If it's okay, go ahead and send it to Mr. Busch. If it isn't, just tear it up and Joanne will think he just didn't answer it."

But Al told me that Mr. Busch had already seen the letter, that it was very well written and very respectful, and in fact Mr. Busch liked it so much that he showed it to everybody. He thought it was really sweet, and he wrote her back and told her that.

My wife likes to say that Mr. Busch really was a nice man who just listened to too many people. We really did like him, even though he wound up firing me twice. Because, hey, he also hired me twice as general manager. The second time, after the Cardinals had won the '67 World Series, he enabled me to be reunited with my family after three years in New York.

I'm not saying Mr. Busch brought me back because of Joanne's letter. But he referred to it when he brought me back.

A few years ago, a reporter asked me for my favorite baseball memory. I told him it was the letter Joanne wrote to Mr. Busch after I was fired the first time. Looking back on that decision now, I'd say it was a pretty good choice.

Devine Daughters

Joanne's letter to Mr. Busch wasn't the only time my girls showed an interest in my work with the Cardinals. As I've said, I got fired in August of '64 and was hired by the Mets a little over a month later. Coincidentally, the Mets came to St. Louis right after that for the last series of the year with the pennant on the line.

Our daughter Janice, who was nine years old at the time, said to Mary, "Mommy, the Mets are playing the Cardinals. That's us against us! Who do we root for?"

I thought that was a pretty good question.

Mary told her, "Honey, I think it's okay if we root for our old team this year, and then our new team next year."

And I thought that was a pretty good answer.

I told you that it was an unpopular trade in St. Louis when I sent Sam Jones to San Francisco for Bill White. It was unpopular in my house, too. Sam Jones was a favorite of my wife and daughters because he always had this toothpick in his mouth. They liked that. The day after I made the deal, Mary and the girls—Joanne,

Janice and Jane—all came to breakfast with toothpicks in their mouths. They were laughing.

But I thought, "Hey, that's not very funny! I'm already taking all this criticism, and now I've got critics at my own breakfast table."

When I was with the Mets and got the offer to come back to St. Louis as general manager, I was pretty sure right away that I was going to take it. I alerted my family that it could happen, and then I flew home to discuss it. I'd been doing that, commuting from New York, for three years.

When we sat down to talk about it, Jane said, "Daddy, you better come home!"

That was kind of typical of Jane. That made it easy to turn down Donald Grant when he called me down to Florida and offered me a piece of the Mets if I'd stay on.

But that didn't mean I was overly important at home just because I was the Cardinals' general manager again. One time when the Cardinals were in New York, the game went on for something like 18 or 19 innings. I didn't make the trip, so I was listening on the radio at home. In about the 12th or 13th inning, I remember Mary saying, "I've got to get the girls to bed. Why don't you turn that down or go listen to it somewhere else?" I think she probably wanted to get some sleep, too.

So I went out to the car parked in the driveway to listen to the radio. I was sitting out there for maybe two hours. The game went on so long, I had to start the car and drive it around so I wouldn't run the battery down.

Bake McBride finally scored the winning run on a wild throw at first base by the pitcher. It was like one or two o'clock in the morning before I could come back inside.

I may have been the general manager at the ballpark, but not at my own house!

In 1968, my first season back as general manager in St. Louis, I got a letter from Janice, who was at college at the University of Arizona. She wrote:

Daddy,

This good friend of mine here at school has a boyfriend who plays on the baseball team. He is a pitcher and is very good, they say.

So I called the coach at Arizona and asked him if he had any big-league prospects.

He said, "Just one, a pitcher named Tim Plodinec."

That was the name that Janice gave me. And we actually drafted Plodinec in the June draft that year. He went to rookie ball and moved up quickly to St. Petersburg in Class A. He made the big leagues for just one game in '72, but it was still a good tip from Janice.

I don't know how many other general managers get players recommended by their daughters! But I've got a pretty good theory: Sometimes you do things that are kind of off the wall. I know that sounds crazy. But it didn't cost us anything to sign Plodinec. He wasn't a bonus player and we didn't have to give up anything for him. I guess the word is, you've gotta get lucky. And I think you've got a better chance of getting lucky in a deal when one of your daughters is scouting.

Anyway, after we drafted Plodinec I got another letter from Janice, congratulating us. She ended that second letter with a P.S.:

Daddy, when you are in St. Petersburg and see Tim, will you please get his girl's home address for me? I lost it

DEFENDING DAD

JOANNE DEVINE AND GUSSIE BUSCH REFLECT ON BING DIVINE

Dear Mr. Busch:

I hope that you won't discard this letter because it appears to be the praise of an elated fan or the rantings of a dissatisfied one. For I am neither of these.

It would simply mean a great deal to me if you would personally take the time to listen to my thoughts.

Of course my father knows nothing of this as he is in N.Y. at this moment, but I'm sure you could guess his reaction as well as I. However, I am sure you have had feelings similar to mine, of wanting so badly to express yourself, and not being able to rest until you have done so.

I would like to assure you that this letter was not written in anger or bitterness. I think that I realize how badly you have wanted to bring a pennant to St. Louis. Perhaps it was because of this one burning desire that you have found yourself saying a hasty remark off guard that was immediately pounced upon by the newspapers.

I can even understand how you must have felt in August when the Cardinals were 7 1/2 games out of first place, with so little time remaining. It was a desperate situation and, perhaps feeling that you had to do something, it was only natural that you would be greatly influenced by someone's damaging sophistry.

But you had lost faith in your organization, and one thing had been forgotten. Many years before the idea of purchasing the Cardinals ever entered your mind and before I was even thought of, there was a man with a dream. He had been with the Cardinal organization for 25 years and this dream had not diminished.

He wanted to contribute something to his hometown and that contribution was to be a pennant for St. Louis. I am in no way belittling your desires, but it does seem unjust that other men, however fine they may be, are reaping the benefits of a situation which my father tried hard to build.

Perhaps you are hoping that your shake-up in the front office gave the players their new incentive. I would be inclined to agree with you. I have watched the Cardinals since August and I have also heard some of their attitudes and beliefs.

It is my opinion the Cardinals do show new "spark," but this spark is not because of whom you brought in but rather because of whom you sent out.

Of course I didn't write this for any reaction nor with the idea that anything could be done. What has already been done is more than enough. A man in your position could never retract any commitments or admit a wrong, if one has been done. I could never hope for this.

Dad will do well in the Mets organization, just as he has done with the Cardinals. New York has brought in a good baseball executive, in the opinion of many. And once more they have brought in a wonderful person, and I speak from 21 years of personal experience.

At the risk of sounding sentimental, I wanted you to know that the Cardinals have always been Dad's first love and, fortunately or unfortunately, this will never change. Good luck to you in all your future endeavors and thank you for listening.

Very sincerely,

Joanne Devine

***

December 29, 1964

Dear Joanne:

As a father myself, I can understand perhaps better than you think exactly how you feel. It must be a great source of pride to your father to have such a loyal supporter in his own family.

I can assure you of one thing—and that is, any decisions about Bing Devine that I have made do not in any manner reflect upon him, either as a person or a man of outstanding character. Bing is one of the finest persons I have ever met—or hope to meet. I have said this publicly, and I'm glad to repeat it to you.

Baseball is not a game that is conducted under any rules of logic since, of necessity, many if not most decisions are based upon judgment. Judgment can be good—or bad, depending upon one's point of view. In this case, the judgment decision was mine. I had to make it—and I did.

Certainly, I did not make it to hurt a man whose character I admire very much. I'm sure your father would agree with much of what I say.

That fact that my decision did not reflect upon Bing's character certainly is indicated by the high esteem that all his friends have expressed upon many occasions since that time.

Let me tell you again how much I appreciate your sharing your thoughts with me. Bing Devine can be proud he has a daughter like you— just as you can be proud you have a father like Bing Devine.

Sincerely,

August A. Busch Jr.

Chapter 9

Front Office Tales

Trading Curt Flood

Curt Flood played center field for the Cardinals for 12 years and was still playing well. But on October 7, 1969, I traded him, catcher Tim McCarver, reliever Joe Hoerner, and outfielder Byron Browne to Philadelphia. But Flood would not report to the Phillies. I called him, and he immediately took the stance of, "Why did you do this? I may not go."

Why did I do that? To get Richie Allen. That part of the deal was controversial, too, because Allen had a reputation of being hard to handle. We also got another infielder, Cookie Rojas, and a pitcher named Jerry Johnson.

Flood never did report to the Phillies. He was protesting the reserve clause, which gave a team the right to control a player's movement once he was their property. That's what Flood objected to, being considered somebody's property with no chance to decide where he would work.

He filed suit against Commissioner Bowie Kuhn in January, 1970. I didn't take it seriously at first. But I should have realized it was serious, because Flood was a strong-thinking personality.

It took six months to complete the deal, because we kept thinking Flood would change his mind. Finally, in April of '70, we sent Willie Montanez, a first baseman, and a right-handed pitcher named Bob Browning to Philadelphia to complete the deal. That was really the end of my involvement in the whole Flood case.

Flood Gates Open

Curt Flood ended up sitting out all of the '70 season and half of the '71 season before Philadelphia "traded" him to Washington. Meanwhile, his case went all the way to the U.S. Supreme Court, which ruled against him in June of '72 by a 5-3 vote, with one abstention.

Even though Flood lost, as time went on and the whole thing unfolded, I felt rather guilty. Especially with what it led to...free agency for major league players at some point in their careers. Free agency didn't come to baseball till 1976. Let's face it, free agency led to the high salaries we have now. And Flood's suit was an important part of the whole process.

I don't think I ever had any negative intent toward Flood's suit. I also justified it by saying it probably would have happened anyway. And the truth of the matter is, it should have happened. When you think about it, the ball club had these players from the time they were signed in the minor leagues, to when they were brought up to the big leagues, for as long as the team wanted to keep them, to do whatever the team wanted with them. The players had no control over their careers.

It's opposed to what the Constitution stands for—freedom. And I recognized that it was wrong. But I didn't know when I made that trade that I was opening the Flood gates.

While the case was going through the courts, Flood came back in '71 and played with Washington. He hit .200 in 13 games and decided to quit. That was his last big-league season. There was some suspicion that he had been blackballed, but I never had anyone in baseball tell me that was happening.

Even though I had traded him, he and I stayed in touch after that. I remember calling and talking to him when he was ill, not too long before he died. Curt Flood was always special to me. He was my first big-league trade, and he was a great player for the Cardinals. Most of all, he was a good person with strong beliefs and the character to act on them.

Releasing Tony La Russa

Tony La Russa was in our minor league system in '77. He was with our Triple A team, which we were moving to Tulsa. A. Ray Smith owned the team and he was building a new stadium in Tulsa. While the stadium was being finished, the team went to New Orleans for a year and played in the Super Dome.

We released Tony as a player. And A. Ray Smith said, "If you're letting him go as a player, do you mind if I keep him as a coach? I'll pay whatever salary's due him as a player."

That's when Tony began studying to be a lawyer. When he came back almost 20 years later to manage the Cardinals, I told him, "I'm the one who sent you to law school."

He didn't seem to think it was very funny. I was just kidding him, and he'd probably say he was going to law school anyhow. But it happened just after I let him go, kind of like the Curt Flood situation that ended up in the Supreme Court.

I look back on those things now, and I wonder, "How do I get in the middle of these things?"

By the way, someone mentioned all of this to Tony last season, and he just laughed and said, "I wasn't mad at Bing for releasing me. Hey, sometimes the truth hurts!"

Which is exactly what I said about my own minor league career, which lasted half a season back in '41.

Signing Pete Vuckovich

In December of '77, we got Pete Vuckovich from Toronto with an outfielder, John Scott, for Tom Underwood and Victor Cruz. Vuckovich was always one of my favorites. He was one of those tough, hard-nosed pitchers.

The thing I remember most about him was trying to get him signed for the next season. He had an agent out of Boston, Bob Woolf. I knew Woolf from previous negotiations, and he was good to work with. The holdup was money. Period. In spring training, Vuckovich hadn't signed, but he was working out with the club. Players did that in those days.

Woolf called me and said, "I can't convince Vuckovich to sign with you. I don't think you're being unfair, but I can't make an impact on him. Why don't you talk to him?"

That was the first time I ever had an agent tell me to see if I could get his player signed for him!

But I called Vuckovich in and told him, "Why don't we meet in an informal environment, maybe go to dinner together, and see if we can work this thing out?"

Vuckovich didn't like that idea. He was suspicious, I guess.

He said, "You're sitting there with a jacket on and a tie on and you're well groomed. I'm wearing an old sweatshirt and jeans. I dress like this all the time and you probably dress like that all the time. You really don't want to go to dinner with me."

I said, "Yeah, I do. Tell you what. You pick the place, and I'll dress to fit the occasion so you won't feel out of place."

He kind of reluctantly said okay.

Dinner wasn't as dramatic as that statement from Vuckovich might lead you to believe. We went somewhere out on the beach, a casual little place. I wouldn't have gone there if he hadn't picked it, but it was fine. I wore something informal. Not a sweatshirt and jeans, but not a coat and tie, either.

We had a good conversation over dinner. And we came to an agreement that enabled me to call Woolf and say, "We got together and here's the deal...."

I told Woolf about the dinner and he laughed. He said, "It's an unusual way to work things out, but I'm glad you worked it out."

So was I. It was just two guys getting better acquainted in a different environment than their normal relationships as a player and a general manager. And after it was all over, both of us came out of it with admiration for each other.

After I left the Cardinals, Whitey Herzog traded Vuckovich along with Ted Simmons and Rollie Fingers to Milwaukee for David Green, Sixto Lezcano, Dave LaPoint and Lary Sorensen. That was the deal that helped both teams get into the '82 World Series.

I've listed Mike Shannon as my number one overachiever, but Vuckovich would also be on that list. He was a real tough competitor. And he looked like a tough competitor, with that Fu Manchu mustache and the way he stared at the hitters.

About three or for years ago, Pittsburgh was in town, and I was up in the press box at Busch Stadium. And in walked Pete Vuckovich. He had a front office job, special assistant to the general manager, and he was dressed nice—not in a sweatshirt and jeans. When we saw each other, we were like two long-lost college buddies getting together and talking about what happened in the interim. I kidded him about being in the front office after what he said to me that time in spring training. We laughed about that, about how things change.

It was neat to see him achieve success in the front office. And the other thing that was pleasing about that whole thing was having an agent call and say, "I can't get through to him. Why don't you talk to him?"

I can tell you that I never had that happen before...or after!

Signing Toothpick Jones

The Vuckovich signing was a strange way to do business. The opposite of that was just as strange, when I was trying to sign Sam "Toothpick" Jones the first time I was the Cardinals' general manager.

I really wasn't even ready to sign Toothpick at the time. I would rather have waited to offer him a contract until we were closer to spring training. But he came up to me after the season and said, "I need it now!"

I said, "Here's the best I can do. Do you want to think about it?"

He said yes, and he went out and walked around the old ballpark, the old Sportsman's Park. He came back in and still wanted to sign.

I said, "Okay, but I just can't do it now."

Jones was a dominant pitcher, but they didn't make that much money and they didn't have an agent. Again, we're not talking about Albert Pujols with a great year, due to get a multiyear contract worth millions of dollars. Back then, the players made a few thousand dollars a year. Toothpick was going to be without income for six months, and he needed the money to get through the winter.

Pitchers for Hitters

Everybody always needs pitching. No question about that. The pennant race during almost any season will prove that.

You need more pitchers on the roster than position players, because you're always subject to pitchers coming up with bad arms. Pitchers are more prone to injury, but they're also easier to teach than hitters. And in a way, pitchers are easier to find because they're easier to scout. You see more of them, even though they only pitch every five days or so. You get to see the starters throw 90 to 100 pitches a game. You can find out how fast they throw with a radar gun. You see them in all situations in almost every game.

But a position player bats three to five times in a game. He might not see a pitch he can do something with. If he does reach base, he might not get to run the bases. When he's in the field, he may not get the ball hit to him very often. That makes it harder to evaluate a position player and project how good he might be. And that's why I say it's harder to find a good everyday player than a good pitcher.

The thought of trading someone who can play every day for someone you can only use every four or five days—that was always tough for me to take. I hated to give up all that activity.

So when I had a chance to get a good position player for a good pitcher, I usually took it. I traded:

• Pitchers Willard Schmidt, Marty Kutyna and Ted Weiand to the Reds for outfielder Curt Flood.

• Pitcher Ernie Broglio to the Cubs for outfielder Lou Brock.

• Pitcher Sam Jones to the Giants for first baseman Bill White.

• Pitcher Vinegar Bend Mizell to the Pirates for second baseman Julian Javier.

• Pitcher Don Cardwell to the Pirates for shortstop Dick Groat.

• Pitcher Rick Wise to the Red Sox for outfielder Reggie Smith.

There are exceptions to this, though. I'd never trade a superstar pitcher, unless I was forced to, like Steve Carlton. And even then I got a top pitcher, Rick Wise, in return. Bob Gibson would have been an exception as well. You wouldn't think of trading him, period. And I never did.

Women in Baseball

Mary Jones was the secretary in the publicity office for the Cardinals when I started in 1939. Mary Murphy was Branch Rickey's secretary then. I hired her niece, Helen Jane Murphy, as my secretary when I was general manager in St. Louis the first time. Then Marilyn Schroeder was my secretary, and I took her to New York with me when I went to the Mets. She stayed with the Mets and became a personal secretary to Joan

Payson, the owner, and later moved to Carolina to help run Mrs. Payson's horse stables. Then Mary Ann Quigley was my secretary when I came back to the Cardinals.

When I went to the football Cardinals, Adele Harris was there. I think her title was director of community relations, but she was involved with everything in the front office, and she helped me out tremendously.

And going back to Triple A in Rochester, I had Anne Dinkwoods assisting me.

You talk about the people with a ball club who work behind the scenes to make you a winner? That's what all of these women did. Without them, you'd have been a loser. You'd have been a goner.

One of the Best

One of my best hires ever was Judy Barada. She was Judy Carpenter when I came back to the Cardinals in '67, and I moved her from another job to the general manager's secretary when Mary Ann Quigley left.

Judy's still with the Cardinals. And they've changed her title since then, which they should have. She's not a secretary. She's the senior executive assistant to the general manager. That's more than just a name change. She's really an adviser, which is what she became to me.

Judy's very strong-minded. She doesn't hesitate to give you an opinion. She speaks up when she thinks you're wrong, or when there's something you should at least think about. In other words, Judy fits the picture of the kinds of people I liked working for me.

Look at all the general managers she's worked for: me, John Claiborne, Whitey Herzog, Joe McDonald, Dal Maxvill, Walt Jocketty. By the time you've worked for that many GMs, you've got to be knowledgeable and you've got to be good at your job.

And she is.

Traveling Secretary

Leo Ward was the traveling secretary when I came back to the Cardinals in '68, and he ran a tight ship. Leo was like a navy chief. He was strict. The players were afraid of him, or respected him. That was back when you could get by running a tight ship. A ballplayer would ask him for 14 tickets, and Leo would decide how many the player would get.

He'd tell the players what to do. But that was before the Players' Association came in. He was the transition from the old traveling secretary to the new. Then Leo died, and Jerry Lovelace took over, followed by Lee Thomas.

Hiring Lee Thomas

I knew Lee Thomas personally and as a major league ballplayer, and I'd see him in town in the off season. He was from St. Louis. He was a star at Beaumont High, and when he quit playing he wanted to come back to St. Louis. We had a conversation and he established that fact.

I tried to find something for him that made sense, and eventually that was traveling secretary for the Cardinals. That's not a job that big-league ballplayers normally move into. But he did more than just make travel arrangements for the ball club. When I had a question on player development, I always valued him as a sounding board. I liked to check with him when I wanted an opinion from someone not so close to me in the baseball office.

Lee was a strong-minded individual. He'd give you his opinion no matter what the consequences, whether he thought you agreed with him or not. That's the kind of person I liked working for me. Now, there are limitations on that kind of person. If the strong judgments are wrong, then you have a problem. Then you have to take some action with the person giving you their poor judgment.

But Lee was a good judge of player talent. He fit the picture very well. And he easily adjusted to anything in his primary job, which was critical.

At the major league level, the traveling secretary is an important person on a ball club. And that's even leaving out the question of travel, hotels and so forth. The job is important because of the relationship you have to have with the players and the understanding you have to have of the life of a player. You're spending half of a season on the road with them. That's three months, plus spring training. And tying into that, you have to have the trust of the players. There's a bonding there that you have to establish.

The traveling secretary has to work with the players and the manager and the general manager. It's not easy. Lee quickly adapted to all of that, and I soon saw that his capabilities went beyond his job responsibilities. I found that he was an excellent judge of ballplayers and baseball talent. As time went on, I placed more confidence in his judgment.

When you get a guy with personality who has the nickname of "Mad Dog," there's a reason for it. He's going to get his job done no matter what...and not worry what people think about him.

Lee did a great job as farm director when Whitey Herzog and Joe McDonald came in to run the Cardinals in the 1980s. And when he got to be general manager in Philadelphia, he did a great job building the Phillies into a World Series team in 1993. After leaving the Phillies, he became assistant to the general manager of the Red Sox. He would make a good general manager again for someone, somewhere. He is still young enough, he's still astute, and he still has his hard-bitten "Mad Dog" personality.

He wants to win and he's not scared of making decisions. I know, because in 1989 he brought me in with him to the Phillies as a special assignment scout. A case of someone I had hired returning the favor to me.

Taking a Hike

When you get right down to it, everbody—no matter what job they're doing—has some idiosyncracies. I hated to lose. And I hated to look bad losing.

When I was general manager of a ball club, I didn't like to look over the shoulder of my manager. But that doesn't mean I always agreed with everything he did, or that I didn't get frustrated when things went bad.

If I was at a game, the way I dealt with that frustration was, I just left. I'd get away. If we were at home, I might just go down to my office. When we still played at old Sportsman's Park, I'd go back up in the right field stands in the upper deck. I knew old Sportsman's Park. I used to sit all over the place with the Knothole Gang when I was a kid.

When we moved to Busch Stadium, I had a box to the left of the press box as you face the field. My wife and daughters were usually up there. When I got upset with the team, I'd go down to the office. Often, I did. My family was used to me leaving. If it was really bad, I'd just leave and drive home.

If we were on the road, sometimes I'd just leave the park and keep going. I'd go back to the hotel. Or sometimes I'd go to the airport and fly to see one of our minor league teams. I'd usually alert the traveling secretary so he could alert the staff. I'd say, "Just tell 'em I'm gone." I didn't want to bother them to get me transportation. I'd get my own. So that night after the ballgame, they just wouldn't see me.

I just didn't want to be around. That's how I dealt with the frustration.

Temper, Temper

At Sportsman's Park, the owner's box was behind the dugout. The general manager had a box right back of the screen behind home plate.

When Frank Lane was the general manager, he'd get so worked up, he'd start screaming! At a ballgame, he was an attention getter—good or bad. You talk about winning and losing and getting upset about it? He really did!

You definitely knew Frank was around. He was an emotional guy. He was extreme emotion. I didn't follow his emotional lead when I became a general manager, but I did take his aggressiveness in making trades, as I said.

Lane would start profanely professing his opinions about the club in his box seat during a game. I'd excuse myself and get up and leave. Later I'd tell him, "You were getting a little worked up, and I didn't want the fans hearing that."

I still do that, get up and leave when I get frustrated, even though I'm just a special assignment scout for the Cardinals. At home, if things get bad when I'm watching them on TV, I'll get up and go to my bedroom. That's better than when I was the general manager when they were on the road. If I was home watching them on TV, if I didn't like what was happening, I'd go outside and kick things in the garage. One time I kicked a little chair in the living room and damaged it. Mary wasn't too happy about that. So from then on, I'd go to the garage.

Room to Work

When I was a general manager, I felt that every department should have the opportunity to do things its own way. Was there the occasional time to step in? Sure, you'd have to step in sometimes. But I thought they should be left to do their jobs their way...if it fit the organizational policy, and if it worked.

Since I grew up in the Cardinals organization and worked in many capacities at so many levels, I recognized the importance of giving an individual the chance to operate without looking over his or her shoulder. I recognized that I would be uncomfortable with my boss looking over my shoulder all the time. And I found that if you left people on their own to do their jobs, you were able to discover plenty about them.

Yes, there were times when things didn't work. When that happened, I didn't want to go off on a fit of anger. I knew that people are never one hundred percent right, or that things never go one hundred percent the way you envision. I always had the feeling that if things were that bad and I couldn't do anything right then to fix it, then I should just get away from it. Sometimes it just fixed itself.

I realized that there's a certain percentage of the time that things just won't work out. The people who work for you can't be right all the time. And you can't be right all the time, particularly when you're dealing with human elements.

There's no textbook for running a baseball team or a sports team of any kind. And even if there were, you're still dealing with personalities, not mathematical figures.

Leave a Message After the Beep

When I came back to the Cardinals in '67, I got an answering machine for the office to take the daily reports from our minor league teams. Answering machines were kind of new then. I don't know if I was the first general manager to use one for that purpose, but I had to be one of the first.

Remember, we didn't have cell phones or e-mail back then. And unless you had a major emergency, you better not be picking up the phone and calling the home office long distance. That was expensive, not like today when it's a few cents a minute. We didn't have all the different long-distance companies competing for business back then. It was just Ma Bell.

So the minor league managers used to send telegrams with reports and highlights from the games. Then somebody in the office would go through them and take down the information.

I did that in '39 and '40 when I first worked as an office boy for the Cardinals after college. We had over 30 minor league teams back then. I'd come in every morning and pick up a handful of these telegrams and go into a meeting room, where there was a blackboard with the standings of all our minor league teams. My job was to update the standings on the board for all of our teams. Then I passed the reports on to whoever was interested in them in the front office—Branch Rickey, for one, and then the people in the player development department.

That was a lot of work for the people in the office, but it was a lot more work for the people sending the reports. I know, because when I went to Johnson City as business manager in '41, I was in charge of sending the telegrams.

Someone with the minor league club had to go out and find a Western Union man after the game. If the telegraph office wasn't open, you had to get up the next day and file your report before you did anything else. That could get complicated when you were on the road, busing to a new town after the game.

The answering machine was a way to simplify all that, to simplify the way you were giving and receiving information. It was modern technology, which seems kind of funny now.

Now, we have our grandson Geoff, driving from St. Louis back to Elon University in North Carolina, calling in every so often from the road on his cell phone, just to let us know he's okay. And if he doesn't call, Mary calls him.

The Best Boss

For all of these names through baseball history that we've talked about, Dick Meyer and Al Fleishman top my list of best bosses. They were two good men and executives who excelled in their trade and were good to me.

Al Fleishman was a great public relations man. And Dick Meyer was Mr. Busch's shadow. That didn't bother Dick Meyer. He just did his job. In fact, he didn't want any attention.

Dick Meyer was on the board of directors of Anheuser-Busch when the brewery bought the Cardinals.

Somebody said, "Hey, Dick Meyer played baseball. He knows about baseball. Let's make him the general manager."

That was the last thing Dick Meyer wanted, as he often told me. Dick had been a catcher. He played semipro ball and was considered good, from what I hear. He was offered a chance to go out with a pro club, but his father wouldn't let him go. He said, "No son of mine will be a tramp ballplayer!"

So for force of family, he never had a chance to play professionally.

Mr. Commissioner?

After I went back to St. Louis, my name came up as the possible commissioner of baseball. William Eckert had been commissioner since he replaced Ford Frick on November 17, 1963. But then Eckert resigned on December 6, 1968, a year after I went back to the Cardinals.

Dick Meyer would go to the owners' meetings for the Cardinals, sometimes with Mr. Busch and sometimes alone. After one owners' meeting—I think it was in Chicago—Dick called me up and said, "Do you have time to come down and see me in the office?"

So I went down to Anheuser-Busch to see Dick. He told me that several of the owners mentioned to him that I should be seriously considered to replace Eckert.

I said, "I think we better forget it. I'm not interested."

Dick said, "You can't just answer me like that and dismiss it in this conversation. You've got to think about it over the weekend."

I told him, "Okay, Dick, I'll think about it over the weekend. But the answer will be the same."

And it was. Even though Dick implied that if I were to acqui-
esce, that would probably result in my becoming commissioner
when he went back to the owners.

I don't think I would have liked it. Commissioners are
involved in so many things that don't include the results of the
games or evaluating players, which to me were the most intriguing
challenges. That's one reason I didn't want to do it.

Going to New York would have been another problem. I'd
already done that for three years when I was general manager of the
Mets, and my family didn't want to move from St. Louis.

So I don't think I ever really second-guessed myself. But in ret-
rospect, you go back in years and say, "How dumb could I be?"

I don't think I came out of it as a brainy guy! But the bottom
line is, I'm just loyal to my original love for the Cardinals. Even
though I ended up getting fired a second time.

The Last One

M y first deal in '58 was for Curt Flood, and my last deal
in '78 was for George Hendrick, both of whom were
pretty good ballplayers. We got Hendrick early in the '78 season
for pitcher Eric Rasmussen, but I didn't have to live with it.
Hendrick didn't make his impact until after that season when I was
already gone. There was a lot of resentment to the deal. Hendrick
came out of San Diego with the reputation of having a bad attitude. People said, "He's a bad guy."

But I said, "The worst problem I heard was that he won't talk
to the public through the media. And I don't know that's so bad."

And that was the only negative, if you want to call it that,
about Hendrick. He refused to go public with his opinions. On
anything.

Looking back, it looks like I took an interest in making deals for guys with attitudes or strong opinions. In 1975, I did bring in another player with a question about his attitude—Willie Davis. I was never that kind of person myself. In school, I was always kind of meek. I was never the one getting into trouble in class. But a guy with an attitude, who was supposedly hard to handle, that didn't bother me...if the guy could play.

Trade Circles

My last trade with the Mets, which Johnny Murphy had to sign off on, was for Tommie Agee. After I came back to the Cardinals, in August of '73, I acquired Agee from Houston for Dave Campbell and cash.

I don't remember much about how Agee played here, because in December of '73, I traded him to Los Angeles for Pete Richert...the pitcher with whom I'd gone to Vietnam for the tour. Proving, I guess, that baseball is a small world!

LEARNING FROM THE BOSS

LEE THOMAS
REFLECTS ON BING DEVINE

I played in Japan during the '69 season. When I came back, I didn't have a job in baseball. That next spring of '70 was the only time I didn't have a job in baseball. Bing called me after that and made me the bullpen coach for the Cardinals in '71 and '72. Then he got me a job managing in the minors. Ken Boyer and I had the Rookie League team in '73, and then I had Class A Modesto in the California League in '74.

But the Cardinals dropped the club, and then I didn't have a job again. I wanted to stay in baseball, and I preferred to stay in St. Louis if I could.

Then Bing called and said, "This is all I have, but take this job until something develops in baseball."

So I went into the front office under Joe Cunningham and sold season tickets. It wasn't easy. You had to wine and dine people to sell them. We sold 1.4 million tickets, and we were horsefeathers for a while there. That was after they made Bing trade Steve Carlton and Jerry Reuss. That really hurt the Cardinals, when both of those guys left. Left-handers don't fall off trees, especially left-handers of that caliber.

When Bing had to trade Carlton, he did get Wise—who was a pretty good pitcher. But he was no Steve Carlton…although he could hit better than Steve.

I think Mr. Busch was really on Bing a lot then. And when Mr. Busch wanted something, he got his way. I got to know Mr. Busch as a traveling secretary, because I did a lot of things for him, too. Bing made me the traveling secretary in '75, and I did that until '80, when Whitey came in and made me the farm director until '88.

When I was traveling secretary, Bing had me in all the baseball meetings. That's not the way it usually goes, but that's probably why I took the job. I had input, mostly into the big-league ball club because that was what I was around the most, obviously.

I wasn't a mole for Bing. Red Schoendienst was the manager, and I got along great with him. But when Bing asked for my opinion on something, I gave him my opinion. As a GM, Bing was very methodical. He gave everybody a chance to voice his opinion. You were not afraid to speak up. He wanted to hear what you had to say.

But he used to get annoyed. One guy in the front office had narcolepsy, and he'd fall asleep in the meetings. He couldn't help it. At first guys would punch him to wake him up. Then guys decided to leave him alone and see how far Bing would go before saying something to the guy.

Let me tell you, Bing intimidated a lot of people. In a good way, not a mean way. They respected him. I know I did. He was very free to give credit to everybody when things went well. And when things didn't, he took the blame. Some of it, he didn't have to. Probably a lot of it, he didn't have to.

But we knew he was the boss. And I learned a lot from him. Number one, he was not afraid to make a move. He'd always tell me, "Don't be wishy-washy." And Bing was very honest, very upfront. I learned to try to be as honest as I could with the players—even when it hurt. He said once they know you're lying or not being straight with them, you're in trouble. They're only going to let you do that once. The second time, they won't trust you. And if you always tell them the truth, you don't have to worry about what you told them the last time.

The third thing he taught me was, "If you don't use your people, then what do you have them around for?" He'd tell me that one all the time. When I got to be a general manager in Philly, I was more hands-on than he was as a GM. The ultimate decision is going to be yours, but get everyone's input on a decision. Then they can't say, "Well, he never asked me."

He'd give people responsibility and trust their judgment, or he'd get new people. And he really liked people who spoke up and stood up for what they believed. Sometimes when these decisions go wrong, those guys who gave you their opinion, you can't find them.

Don't let him kid you about all those other people being the ones who really made those decisions that worked out. It's awfully easy to sit there and say what someone should do. It's awfully easy for Keane to say, "Go ahead and get Brock," or Hutchinson to say, "Go ahead and get Flood." In the end, Bing had to make the final decision. And that's not easy.

Believe me, until you sit in that seat and have that responsibility, you can't know what it's like.

Chapter 10

Fired Again

Taking the Rapp

Red Schoendienst retired as manager after the 1976 season, and I hired Vern Rapp, who had been in the Reds system. To some extent, he had a problem like Solly Hemus. He came in with all these ideas and applied it all, and he didn't ask for a lot of help. Rapp and Hemus didn't understand that to be a good manager, you have to not only be the boss, but you have to have a good working relationship with the players.

We were 83-79 in Rapp's first season in '77. But the next year, we started out 6-11, and I replaced him. Jack Krol stepped in temporarily, while I was hiring Kenny Boyer, and went 1-1. We were 62-81 the rest of the way with Boyer. The next year we did a lot better, 86-76. But we were just third in the National League East behind Pittsburgh, which won 98 games, and Montreal.

In '78, we dropped to 69-93 and finished fifth in the division. I had a bad premonition of the future.

The Ultimatum

After Mr. Busch was replaced as head of the brewery by his son, August Busch III, I remember coming to spring training in '78 and meeting August at the house they had on the beach in St. Petersburg, Fla.

In effect, August indicated in a non-belligerent manner: "Well, you know, the buck stops somewhere else now. So we'll have to see some quick success." I remember the meeting with him, not the confrontation verbatim. But the message was very clear: "The buck stops at the same level but with a different person, and we'll have to see what happens."

He was implying that if we didn't achieve success rather quickly, and as fast and as often as we could, someone would suffer the consequences. That someone was me. I had never assumed otherwise for any franchise where I worked. But I remember him emphasizing that fact, which was not a surprise to me.

Dick Meyer still worked for Mr. Busch, and Al Fleishman was still Mr. Busch's publicity man, but when we didn't win in '78 there was nothing anyone could do.

Another Goodbye

When you look at that period when I came back to the Cardinals, from '69 to '78, the club didn't do that well. While we were competing and coming close earlier in the '70s, toward the end of the decade we were also-rans. That got to Mr. Busch again and brought about my second separation.

After the '78 season, I got a call from Al Fleishman. Al tipped me off, just like the first time. And I didn't waste time arguing, just like the first time I got fired. But this time, I wasn't shocked. I'd recognized the way the club had gone throughout the end of the '70s. I realized it might happen. I wasn't in any long-term contract. The longest I ever had was two years.

Dick Meyer was still Mr. Busch's right-hand man, but he was in the hospital. Afterward, Dick told me he had talked to Mr. Busch and said, "I don't agree with it, but if you're going to get rid of Bing Devine, I'd like to be there."

Mr. Busch said, "Yeah, but you're in the hospital."

And Dick said, "Yeah, but I'm up and around. We can do it from my hospital room."

He had that kind of a close relationship to me. I've said before, he was the best boss I've ever had. Anywhere. So when Al Fleishman called me the night before, he told me that Dick didn't want me to get fired without both of them—meaning Dick and Mr. Busch—being there. So we all met at Dick's room at Lutheran Hospital. It was short—not a lot of conversation. It doesn't take long to get fired, let's face it.

Then Mr. Busch left.

Dick said to me, "Well, we both did the best we could. At least we got you back for another World Series in '68 after you missed the one in '64 and the next one in '67."

I didn't take it as hard as the first time. Hey, getting fired is getting fired. After it's happened once, the second time you're prepared for it. Especially when Al Fleishman gave me a heads-up the night before. Then you know not to go in there and try to argue about it. It's already been decided.

I couldn't be mad at Mr. Busch. He brought me to the big leagues. He made me a general manager for seven years. He brought me back as general manager for another 11 years. And I recognized that it was part of the game. I'd fired managers and traded ballplayers. People get separated in baseball. That's the business. You have to put it behind you and move on.

Seventies Postmortum

What went wrong in the '70s? Things just didn't work out, that's all I can say. We had some good teams and we came close. We finished second in our division three times—in

'71, '73 and '74—and we were third in '77. We were fourth in '70 and '75 and fifth in '78, my last year.

The problem wasn't the manager, at least for the first several years, because the manager was Red Schoendienst. And he was great. Very seldom is the manager the problem anywhere. Whenever I had to replace a manager, I always said I didn't get him enough help. And I meant it. Most of the time, either the players aren't capable of the job or injuries enter into the picture. Sometimes, the anticipation of the way you put it all together just doesn't measure up to the results.

In companies, a lot of personnel movement occurs because the company's not successful. In baseball, you get fired if your players don't do well on the field. Player talent is a fairly difficult thing to evaluate. It's different from making a product that's the same all the time. To put together a group of players to perform the way you think they could or should, that's hard to predict. Take the Cardinals in 2003. I don't think Walt Jocketty did anything different in how he ran his operation. He tried to put things together the way it had worked for him in the past. But it wasn't working this time around.

People ask me about having to trade Steve Carlton for Rick Wise before the '72 season. Yes, I think Carlton would have made a difference in our record in the '70s. He was such a dominating pitcher. While a pitcher only plays every fourth or fifth day, it has a bearing on the pitching staff and the club when you lose a dominant guy like that. That first year, though, Wise was not a bad pitcher for us. He was 16-16. We got him in February, 1972, and we traded him in October, 1973. Because of that trade we acquired Reggie Smith. You hated to trade a productive pitcher. But everything else being equal, if you could get a guy who plays every day for a guy who plays every four or five days, you do it.

I also had to trade Jerry Reuss two months later, in April of '72. Mr. Busch didn't like him, either, but I know it was more dramatic that he didn't like Carlton. We got Scipio Spinks for Reuss, a starting pitcher for a starting pitcher. But Spinks got hurt shortly after we traded for him—running the bases, as I recall. So that became a lost cause.

Looking at the '70s, it didn't help that Mr. Busch made us trade what would have been our No.1 and No. 2 pitchers for the rest of the decade. But you know what? The owner has that right, and you just have to work around it. That's the nature of the business.

Settling Up

In '64 Mr. Busch—again through Dick Meyer's intervention—paid me through the calendar year. I got fired in August that year and hired by the Mets in September. That was the first time in my life I've ever received two paychecks at the same time. It wasn't a big thing. It wasn't a huge salary as we know salaries today. But it did help ease the sting from a material standpoint. The second time I was fired, I was under contract through the same period beyond the end of the season. It wasn't long.

I never had an agent. I was treated very fairly. I had no complaints. I had two pretty good guys in my corner, Dick Meyer and Al Fleishman. Both were about as close as you could get to Mr. Busch. I never made a case for myself when we did my contract. Whatever was offered I took and just went about my business. I never renegotiated my contract with anybody. That went for Mr. Busch and all the other clubs included. The only thing that was close to a renegotiation was when I left the Mets and Donald Grant called me down to Florida to talk to me about staying. I don't want to make this sound like a sob story, but that was the only time I was put in a position by ownership to negotiate a better deal. And I didn't do it!

That was because of a real love for a club, the Cardinals, and my family back here in St. Louis.

Mr. Busch's Attorney

When I got fired the second time, it wasn't any great secret that Lou Susman had a hand in it. He was Mr. Busch's lawyer, and he influenced Mr. Busch, who perhaps didn't need a great deal of influence to make the change.

As I heard the story, when they had the meeting to discuss what to do with me, Mr. Busch said, "Where do we go from here?" That's when John Claiborne's name came up. Susman knew something about Claiborne, and I know Susman recommended Claiborne. I don't think Susman had any hate toward me. I don't want to give too much credit or discredit to him for what happened to me. Even though I know my family disagrees with me on that. (My daughter Janice said she once tried to pay a waiter to spill coffee on Susman when she realized they were at the same restaurant.)

I look at it like this. Susman happened to be close to Mr. Busch. How much influence he had, I don't know. I don't want to make a big deal about that.

Replaced by a Protégé

It was kind of an odd situation when John Claiborne replaced me. He was out of baseball that year. He and I had been talking a lot on the phone about how he wanted to get back in the game. This went on for a period of weeks and months during the '78 season. And it went on afterward, even up until I got fired. So I was giving him recommendations on the side for other jobs while Susman was pushing for him to replace me.

What a strange situation. I'm trying to help a guy get a job in baseball, and he ends up with mine! John and I talked about that afterward. I said, "Through no involvement by you and no knowledge by me, you end up here."

As it turned out, he knew just before they fired me that he would be the guy replacing me. John didn't tell me. He later apologized for that.

MY MENTOR

JUDY CARPENTER BARADA REFLECTS ON BING DEVINE

I came to the Cardinals in March of '67. I was working in group sales. And then I was working for Jim Toomey in the public relations department when Bing returned after the '67 World Series.

Bing's secretary then was Mary Ann Quigley, who is Lee Thomas's sister-in-law. She was getting married and moving to Minneapolis. She and I were good friends, and she thought I should apply for her job. Actually, there were other people who applied who were there longer than I was. I thought they deserved it more than I did, so I didn't apply.

One day, the team was playing at home and some of us were just waiting for the game to start. They didn't start until eight o'clock back then.

Bing came over and said, "Mary Ann tells me that you want to talk to me."

I said, "Well, noooo…"

And he said, "Well, I want to talk to you! Now come on over to my office."

When we got there, Bing said, "Mary Ann tells me that you're the best, and I want to have the best. But you have to apply for it."

I told him, "Thank you, that's very flattering, but I feel bad because I think other people have been here longer and deserve it more."

Bing said, "Well, if you're the best, you're the person I want. And you should apply."

And so I did, and I got the job.

Looking back, Bing touched a lot of people who came out of that place and went on to do other things. People like Lee Thomas and Bob Harlan. And Bing had a lot to do with our success. Bing was the one who encouraged me to read the Blue Book, which is what they call the book of baseball rules for off-the-field stuff. He'd say to me, "What's an option assignment? You should learn about all this."

He was my mentor.

Back then everybody was afraid of him. I wasn't, because I saw him every day and knew that he was the biggest cream puff in the world! But he has a demeanor about him. He knows what he wants to say and he says it. People misinterpreted that. He's abrupt. People who weren't around him a lot would say, "He's not listening," or "He doesn't care what I think." That wasn't true, but he came across that way sometimes because he could be abrupt.

And he would get mad. Not often, though, and most people never saw it. But I remember one time in his office, when he had the door closed and was mad about something. I heard him yelling in there, and I went in to see what was wrong. There were newspapers everywhere. He read everything that came through here, and he would stack the newspapers in a closet, but he'd thrown them all over the place this time because he was so angry.

I started to tidy up, and he yelled, "Don't pick them up! I will pick them up, but I just have to get through this."

So I just went out and closed the door. You have to remember that there was so much pressure on him. Back then the general manager in baseball was in charge of everything. The players, public relations, tickets, sales, everything. It got to be too overwhelming for a general manager.

One time Bing said, "I don't even have time to go down to the minor leagues and look at the players."

I remember when Montreal wanted to hire him away from here. Montreal was the first club to split the job and go to one person for the baseball side and one person for the business side. The Expos offered Bing a three-year deal to be the general manager and just deal with the baseball side. Bing told Mr. Busch—old Mr. Busch, August Busch Junior—about the offer, because he had to get permission to talk to another club. Mr. Busch countered. And Bing decided to stay here. Mary didn't want to go, and neither did Bing, really. They were thrilled to stay in St. Louis.

But August Busch III had some say in this, too. And he said, "Nobody down at the brewery gets a three-year deal." So they only gave Bing two years on his new contract. This was after he turned Montreal down, so he had no leverage then.

I said, "Bing, if they can knock a year from the contract, that worries me."

Mr. Busch was good to me. The whole Busch family treated me well. But my observation is that Mr. Busch was ticked off that Bing would consider leaving. I think that always bothered Mr. Busch. It was around a year and a half later that they let Bing go.

I felt bad for Bing because he, and any general manager, has to do things that his bosses want him to do. It was pretty hard for him when he replaced Red Schoendienst as manager.

Bing was interviewing other managers, Vern Rapp and Joe Altobelli, and he didn't want the press to know. So we were picking these people up at the airport in Bing's car. I was driving. He'd talk to them in the back, so nobody would find out that they were in town. We would take them to Grant's Farm, and Bing would prep them on who they would meet. Mr. Busch would be there, and Lou Susman, who was Mr. Busch's attorney. He had a great deal of influence over Mr. Busch.

And it was really hard when Bing had to trade Steve Carlton and Jerry Reuss, our two best pitchers. It was in spring training, and we were close to getting both of them signed. I mean, real close. And they wouldn't take the last offer. It wasn't even worth fighting for, but for some reason they both wanted a little bit more. Mr. Busch was at a point in his life where his health was not the best. And Mr. Busch just said, "Trade the SOBs!"

It was my first spring training. I'd never gotten to go to Florida with the team before. And I was thinking, "What? We're getting rid of these two guys because of this?" But Bing had to trade our two best pitchers. You can't replace guys like that. That hurt us all through the '70s, and Bing took the rap for that.

Bing's a company man. He's one of the most loyal people you'd ever want to meet. Sometimes I'd get upset with some of his friends. Bing is so loyal that he doesn't see anybody's faults, and I think some people took advantage of that. I'd say that if Bing has a fault, it's that he is totally loyal. Now, if he doesn't like you, he has no use for you. But if he likes you, he'll do anything to help you. Look what he did for Mike Shannon. He helped save his life when Mike had that kidney disease. Well, Dr. London, Stan London, saved his life. But Bing got him into the broadcast booth when he couldn't play any more.

I know I learned a great deal from working for Bing. I learned how to be professional by watching him, how he handled things, how he talked to people in certain situations. I know how to deal with people, but I have a tendency—because of the Italian in me—to be a little fiery. He could be just as mad as me about something, but he could control it. He taught me to sit back and look at a situation and analyze it. And *then* talk. Instead of barging in, which was my gut reaction. I learned from him how to pick my spots. Some things are not worth fighting for.

And he made me feel like part of his family. Mary used to take me with her to go shopping. She and Bing are just wonderful people.

Here's how loyal Bing is. My brother, Bob Carpenter, and two of his friends were at spring training one year. They were teenagers, and we all drove back from Florida with Bing. He wanted us to help with the driving, although we probably drove him crazy in the car.

We were in Tennessee somewhere and we had the radio on, and we heard that Gil Hodges had died.

Bing said, "Take me to an airport. I've got to get on a plane. You take my car to St. Louis."

That's what we did. We were near Chattanooga or somewhere, and Gil Hodges died and Bing had to be there at the funeral.

The St. Louis baseball writers gave me their "Good Guy Award" this year at their banquet. When Bing found out, he said, "Do you want me to write your speech?"

He's a great writer, so I said, "I might! But I'll give it a try first."

When I got done with it, I sent him a copy with a note: "To my dear friend and my mentor. I know you'll be honest with me. Too long? Too schmaltzy? Too anything?"

I still really trust his opinion. He is just so professional.

Chapter 11

Life Goes On

Joining the Giants

After Mr. Busch fired me the second time, I went to work the next year as a scout for Spec Richardson with the San Francisco Giants. He was a friend of mine, and I think he hired me more than anything so he could have a friend around to talk to.

I gave Spec his first job in baseball. He was my concessionaire in Columbus, Georgia, a Class A team. I went there right out of the service in 1946 and '47. Spec was a businessman, basically, and a nice Southern gentleman. You felt like you could trust him more than you could trust yourself.

Eventually he was made the general manager of the Giants for a couple years. To an extent, he was placed in the wrong position. He would have been better suited as the business manager. He wasn't a typical general manager because he wasn't a great baseball evaluator. He had no real background for the field. Period.

His real talent was in the business end. But you could trust him greatly. There was no feeling that he'd double-cross you.

When Spec was in Houston, Roy Hofheinz, the owner, knew he had somebody he could trust implicitly. But after Spec hired me with the Giants, we spent time in the minors looking at players. I'd go in for meetings in San Francisco. We'd watch the Giants if they were at home, and I got my fill of the ballpark there, Candlestick Park. People ask me if it was the worst big-league ballpark. And the answer is…yes. There was the wind and the cold, and it was murder to get to and from. You'd hit traffic if you'd drive out from downtown or in from out of town. It didn't matter. But the odd thing about Candlestick was the wind. It would swirl.

I worked for the Giants for one year. And with that ballpark, that was enough.

Off to Montreal

After a year as a special assignment scout for the Giants, I moved on to Montreal for two years as vice president of player development. This was 1980 and '81. John McHale hired me. We had never worked together, like Spec Richardson and I did. But I got to know John when I was general manager of the Cardinals and he was general manager of the Expos. We'd talk on the phone, doing business, and see each at the winter meetings. He was a nice man and a good friend.

When John hired me with the Expos, I wasn't on the road all the time scouting. I lived in a downtown hotel anytime I was in Montreal. The Expos gave me a car to use. Because of the time differential with the East Coast and the Midwest, I'd put the Cardinals game on the car radio on KMOX—which at 50,000 watts you could pick up just about anywhere—as I drove back to the hotel.

One time, I noticed a nice-looking park when I was driving around. There were a lot of people there, a lot of activity. I didn't think I'd have to be afraid of being sabotaged or ambushed in the car. So I'd drive around, listening to the Cardinals game, and sometimes I'd stop by this park.

People would wave and come up to the car window and say, "Everything all right? Can we help with anything?"

I'd say, "I'm just listening to a ballgame."

One time I happened to mention this to John McHale, how I'd stop by the park and how friendly the people were.

He said, "Where did you say that park is?"

I told him. And he said, "Yeah, that's a friendly park. It's a gay park."

So that was the end of that. I found somewhere else to stop when I drove around listening to the Cardinals.

The Evolving Game

Baseball has changed in a lot of ways since I first went to work for the Cardinals in 1939. One of the big changes is artificial turf fields. I'm sure it has some impact on balls getting past the fielders and through the infield, but the main thing is it's so tough on the body. And artificial turf is even worse in hot climates. When it's 90 degrees up in the press box, it's 100 or 120 degrees on the turf. When it's your home field where you play half of your ballgames, playing on artificial turf takes something out of you over the course of a season.

The other big change in the game is free agency, which has lead us to the big contracts and the uneven ability of clubs to hire free agents or keep their own free agents. I don't know about decade to decade, over a 50-year period, if the ballplayers themselves have changed. Their conditioning has changed, for certain. Players used to go to Hot Springs, Arkansas, to boil out before the season. They used to start to get in shape in February for the start of spring training. Now they condition year-round. Now they're ready for spring training at the first of the year. Players don't need an off-season job to supplement their salary any more. So when spring training comes, many of them are already in baseball shape.

I think the talent all around is better now—I really do. Again, I think that's because of conditioning.

The DH

I was for the designated hitter in 1972 when it first came in. It just made sense to me to help present a more interesting game. With the DH, you didn't have a definitively weak spot in the lineup. It added something to fan interest. But I think both the American and National Leagues should be playing the same way. It's too bad they haven't come to some kind of agreement, instead of just the American League using it.

I was never very steeped in tradition. If there was something new and better from a fan standpoint, so be it. With the DH, it's arguable. It keeps older ballplayers active. But it's understandable why people have feelings on the matter one way or the other.

I guess I'm just offensive-minded, maybe because I couldn't hit myself!

Possibly Pinstripes

When I was with the football Cardinals in '81 or so, Clyde King called me and asked if I'd like to go to work for George Steinbrenner. I was making pretty good money with the football team. But I went down to Florida to meet with Clyde King, and briefly with Steinbrenner, over lunch.

We met at George's hotel. He said, "We've got an opening as director of player development or in scouting. I'll leave you with Clyde, and you two talk about it."

So he got up, and Clyde talked about their offer. It was considerably less than the amount I was making with the football Cardinals. I thought a lot about it and I turned it down. The differential was just too great. I regretted that, but I couldn't justify it.

I would have enjoyed working for George, even though the stories have surfaced about people working for him under difficult circumstances. Working for strong people never bothered me. I respect George Steinbrenner, and I admire him and what he's accomplished.

David Glass

My friendship with David Glass dates back to my days as the general manager of the Cardinals. At that time, he was a lifelong fan of the club. His association with Wal-Mart Stores, eventually becoming chief executive, preceded his interest in acquiring ownership of the Kansas City Royals.

When David first considered buying a big-league baseball team, at his request I set up a meeting with knowledgeable baseball people in St. Louis. He wanted to ask questions and get advice about purchasing a club. After he bought the Royals, we would have conversations from time to time, sometimes only commiserating about our respective teams. We would, and still do, discuss major league teams and players. Not that I was an important part of his organization at any time.

He did question me about Tony Pena as a managerial candidate. I really did not know Pena except as a capable receiver in the big leagues. But I did make some inquiries about him, all of which were positive. So I relayed the information to David: in effect, that Pena should make an excellent manager. And he certainly has. He was named the American League Manager of the Year in 2003.

With David's longtime background as a fan of the game and astute financial experience with Wal-Mart, he has all the requirements to be a successful baseball owner. He knows player talent, too. And not just players. He's surrounded himself with expert personnel in all categories of a baseball operation. The success of the 2003 Royals attests to those facts.

He fits the category of other ownership types I've mentioned, such as Dick Meyer, Gussie Busch, Joan Payson, Donald Grant and George Steinbrenner. Despite having different personalities, they are all strong decision makers with an intense desire to win. That means winning on the field and with their finances.

With David, in addition to his qualifications, he's a nice man and a gentleman with a sense of humor. The best way I can put it is that Stan Musial is a great ballplayer and a nice man; David Glass is a great executive and a nice man.

Forming the Sports Commission

I joined the St. Louis Sports Commission when it was founded in 1989 and stayed involved for 10 years, until I went back to baseball to scout for the Astros. The Sports Commission was trying to build something from the ground up. Our mission was to attract major sports events to St. Louis, to help build new facilities and to help the region economically by bringing in major sporting events. But we also wanted to help all the existing local sports, from the grass roots on up to the professionals. And I think we built a pretty good foundation.

We held the 1994 U.S. Olympic Festival, which broke all the records for attendance and revenue. The Sports Commission also helped win the rights to the NCAA Women's Final Four and the Men's Final Four. They've held or are going to hold national championships in wrestling, figure skating and hockey in St. Louis.

Our first executive director was Mike Dyer. Mike's the best young executive I've ever been associated with. As you've seen, that covers a lot of territory. He had a strong opinion, the willingness to take a stand, a strong work ethic and never shifted the blame. Sound familiar?

My job was to give some credibility to Mike and to help him through the early days of creating some top-level associations. And he went on to bigger and better things. He was a vice president of special events for the National Basketball Association, and he is now with Sony. Frank Viverito replaced Mike as executive director, and Frank's done a good job taking it from there.

When Mike and I started 15 years ago with the Sports Commission, our biggest problem was developing credibility. The

Sports Commission was something new and different for St. Louis. I don't think people questioned that there could be a need, but just the priority of sports in the community. It was the age-old question of, "How important could it be when we've got the problems of education and drugs and all of that?"

Over the years, the commission has proved its value.

Once a Cardinal...

O bviously, I owe a debt of gratitude to the present Cardinals ownership. They believed I was not too old or too far removed to make a contribution from a player-evaluation standpoint when they hired me again in January of 2000 as a special assignment scout.

I firmly believe the best days of the St. Louis Cardinals franchise are still ahead. Present ownership is rooted in St. Louis and committed to winning. They have a talented and aggressive general manager in Walt Jocketty and a knowledgeable and aggressive field manager in Tony LaRussa. The surrounding personnel are dedicated as well. Also, a much-needed new stadium has finally been approved. And most of all, they have a solid foundation to the franchise in the fans, recognized as the best in baseball. Their enthusiasm and support are great assets to the success of the team on the field.

My own upbringing as a Cardinals fan began with my father taking me to see the first world championship in 1926. No matter what I've done over the years, my background as a fan has stayed with me. And it is still a huge part of my life. That can be confirmed by my direct association with the St. Louis club on four different occasions:

• In '39, when I was first hired as an office boy at old Sportsman's Park.

• In '46, when I came back from the navy in World War II to become general manager of our farm club in Columbus, Georgia.

• In late '67, when I left New York to become general manager again.

• And in January of 2000, when I returned this last time as a special assignment scout.

Which goes to prove, as I've said before: You can take me away from the Cardinals, but you can never take the Cardinals away from me.

A GREAT PIECE OF ADVICE

WALT JOCKETTY REFLECTS ON BING DEVINE

I did not know Bing before I came here after the '94 season. I may have met him, but I did not really know him that well. Since I arrived here, I've had some conversations with him and had breakfast with him. I was very interested in what he had to say, talking about what it was like when he was running things. Certainly things are much different today. The economics are a lot different today. But still, he's been an asset and a resource.

You know, he gave me a great piece of advice. I think it was after the '99 season. We had struggled for a couple of years. I had all of our scouts together for some meetings, and we were trying to decide what direction we were going to go. There was always a concern about giving up young players in trades.

And Bing told me, "You have to be concerned about the future, but you also have to be more concerned about the present. If you have to give up two or three young kids—who may not be able to play for several years—to get help for your team now, you have to do it."

What it did was it kind of pushed me over the edge, and made me think that we did have to give up these young guys. Because we were really agonizing over some of these deals. That was the year we really had a busy off season. We traded for Darryl Kile, Dave Veres, Fernando Viña, Pat Hentgen. So that piece of advice from Bing was very important.

I also remember him telling me then that I'd regret it if we didn't make the deal for Jim Edmonds. That was tough, because we were giving up a guy who'd been our best pitcher the year before, Kent Bottenfield. I guess that's one thing you do as a general manager. You've got a pretty good idea of what you want to do, but you're looking for support. Bing is still that voice of experience. The game may have changed, but the decision process and the things that you have to look for to make up your team don't change. That's why we hired him as a special assignment scout in January of 2000. He looks at the National League clubs and gives me his input. And he also has gone out and looked at a couple of our minor league clubs.

He's an interesting man, a very interesting man. Bing told me about how he made the Brock deal. He said he told Johnny Keane about this deal they could make, and Johnny said, "What are you waiting for?" I know he gives Johnny credit for making that deal, but that wasn't Johnny telling him what to do. This was something that was Bing's idea, and Johnny supported him.

It's easy being a number two guy and giving your advice. Then you go home and go to sleep. It's the number one guy who gets the advice and goes home and can't sleep, agonizing over his decision. Look at all the years Bing did that.

One of the best compliments that I've received is when someone told me I reminded him of Bing Devine. I think that's a great compliment for a general manager, to be compared to someone of his stature.

Chapter 12

From Diamond to Gridiron

The Other Cardinals

When I was fired the second time in 1978, I never thought I'd ever be associated with the St. Louis Cardinals again. I was wrong. Just three years later, in 1981, I moved across the hall at Busch Stadium and spent the next five years with the St. Louis football Cardinals.

I knew Bill Bidwill, the owner of the football Cardinals, pretty well. Their offices were right across from ours at Busch Stadium, which we shared with them when I was with the baseball Cardinals.

Bill knew me from across the hall during my days with the baseball Cardinals. He was familiar my background and knew that I had a good relationship with the media and with the public. I think he felt a friendlier relationship was needed between him and the public. And it was.

Bill hired me right here at our house in Ladue. He came out and sat in a chair in the TV room. I was prepared to take a job with his team as vice president of public relations.

When we started to discuss that, he said, "I made up my mind that I'm not going to make you a vice president."

Then he smiled at me and said, "I've decided that you're going to be the president of the team."

Through the years there's been a lot of criticism of Bill Bidwill, in St. Louis and in Phoenix. But not from me. He did everything he said he was going to do with me, and for me—and more. I didn't have anything to do with the club on the field. But I had the benefit of being with the club when they had a successful season, which was fairly infrequent. I was there when the Cardinals made the playoffs in '82 and went to Green Bay. That was a lot of fun, even though we lost up there, 41-16.

I was more involved with administration. Adele Harris was my main contact. She was great.

Knowing Bill Bidwill

What people don't realize about Bill Bidwill is that he was a very kind, generous, caring person. But he seemed very cautious about exposing that side of himself. He didn't want people to know that. And if they did, he didn't want it discussed.

I'd be walking with him down the street and we'd have a random meeting with someone I knew. I'd introduce Bill, and the first thing he'd do was throw out a one-liner. He'd always tell a joke right away when he met someone. I think he did that to feel more at home, to make people see a different side of him. But it also kept him from having to make any conversation about himself.

I always felt that Bill had an inferiority complex, or some kind of complex. He also put on a lot of weight back then. That became a point of comment for media and fans. And that really bothered him. He was very sensitive about his weight. That's something that impressed me over a period of time.

One year after the football season and before spring training, I thought about getting back into baseball. I had an offer to go back to the Expos. So I told Bill, and we had a discussion about my contract status. We had an agreement about my salary when I joined the club, but we never put it in writing. We both just never got around to it.

So Bill said, "What's our deal?"

I said, "Well, I was going to be paid through this year."

And he said, "Whatever you tell me the deal is, that's our deal."

He was great about it. Then he asked me when I was planning to leave.

I said, "I thought I'd leave after we got set up in training camp in July."

And his reply, one of his one-liners, was: "Why wait?"

I thought about it, and I just laughed and said, "You know what? You're right."

Some people might think he was being bitter or rude, but he wasn't. He didn't say it critically or sarcastically. What he meant was, "If you want to be back in baseball, if that makes you happy, you should go ahead and do it now." That may not be how it sounds when you hear it. But it's easy to misread him if you don't know him. It's hard to get to know the real Bill Bidwill. He's very guarded. He's almost afraid to let people know that he's nice. He made sure people never knew the real Bill Bidwill, even if that meant people had a negative opinion of him.

When I started working with him, working on ways I thought I could contribute, I got to know him better than I thought I would. The real Bill Bidwill had never been exposed to me before that, either.

Costas the Critic

When Bob Costas was a very young announcer at KMOX Radio, before he established his reputation, he was kind of sassy in his comments about the football Cardinals. I remember sitting in a meeting with the club's top brass, particularly Bill Bidwill and Joe Sullivan, who ran the football operation. They were upset with Costas being so flippant.

They were saying, "Why's he saying this stuff about us?" It really bothered them.

I said, "Well, why don't I set up a meeting with Costas? You can all get to know each other and develop a better relationship."

They said okay. So I called Costas and he said, "Fine." And he came over to the office. The meeting was just Bidwill, Sullivan, Costas and me. We sat down, and I tried to set the stage for the meeting and the discussion. When I got done talking, Costas said something about what he'd said on the air and why he'd said it. He was very conciliatory, trying to explain what he meant.

Bidwill and Sullivan just sat there and listened to him. They never said a word. Nothing. It was very awkward.

When the meeting was over, it just hit me that Bill and Joe really didn't have anything to say to fit the picture. As far as their participation in the conversation was concerned, it was a wasted effort.

Costas and I later discussed it a few times, the lack of results, the lack of anything beneficial that came out of it. It didn't even result in a debate or a critique. It was, "Hi, how are you?" And nothing else.

When it was finally over I thought, "What a great idea—that didn't work!"

Silent Bill

My daughter Janice says I told her that when I worked for Bill Bidwill, he once went a year without speaking to me, that he just sent memos to me or communicated through a third party. If I told her that, I was exaggerating. But you could go for days and not have him speak to you directly.

One time when Bud Wilkinson was coaching the team, I said to him, "Hey, Bud, Bill just came by and didn't say anything. He just ignored me."

Bud said, "I've been through that, too. I've passed him in the hall and he didn't say anything, not even any recognition that I was there. But don't worry about it. When he has something on his mind, that's the way he is. He's just preoccupied."

That's exactly what it was. And the other thing was, as I mentioned, he wasn't good at small talk. So when he wasn't ready to talk, he wasn't going to talk. You weren't going to coax him into a conversation.

I don't remember having any kind of confrontation with him. And I never heard him raise his voice. To anyone. He usually showed his dissatisfaction by being very terse, if he said anything at all.

I really think that his personality is why people in St. Louis have certain ideas about him. But leaving out all these little personal items, or quirks, he was a fair guy.

At least he certainly was to me.

Football vs. Baseball

Back then with the football Cardinals, Joe Sullivan was the driving force in the actual field activities, the man who actually led the way. I was completely administrative. I didn't come in with any football knowledge, and nobody there was under the impression that I did.

I think a lot of fans would say, "Gee, I know more about this than I thought I did." I didn't think like that. In fact, my first year there I made an effort to develop a better relationship with the various scouts. I wanted to relate football to baseball, some part of it that I knew. And that part was scouting and player evaluation.

At the start, I had to fight off the habit of thinking I knew more than I did. I relate that to fans and media thinking that they know more about something than they had reason to.

I found a real differential in scouting between football and baseball. In baseball, you can always find somebody to scout. You could see a game of some value every day of the week. High school, college, minor league, major league. In football, you're tied down to 10 or 11 weekends. That's it.

So I found out about how the football scouts used team practices for evaluation and how they developed relationships with the college coaches, particularly the assistants who work with players at their positions. It was interesting to see how much value the football scouts received from watching practice.

Don't get me wrong, I still think it's best to see how players perform in games. There's nothing to take the place of seeing people participate when they actually have an opponent. The next best thing is to see them do the things in practice that they do in the games.

In any kind of scouting that I've been around, it's very easy to recognize the importance of speed with any player. But I'm basically talking about speed of movement, how running speed by itself can almost make you a prospect.

In baseball, you're scouting players going to the minor leagues for development. In football, you're looking for someone who can help your team immediately, or someone who can at least be a backup and fit in well enough to gain experience to get to that level. You're not looking at anyone to go out and play in the minors for two or three years to be ready. And that's a major difference in scouting between football and baseball.

Know Your Limitations

On draft day with the football Cardinals, I was in the room sometimes. I had a blanket invitation to be there. I never said anything when they were deciding on a player, even if I thought I knew something about it. And sometimes I probably thought I did!

They never said, "Well, we can't make up our mind. Let's see what Devine wants to do."

I never expected them to do that, and they never did. Hey, I thought—and I think—I had a reason to know about a baseball

player. I didn't think I had a reason to know about a football player. I always knew where I belonged.

Why They Lost

When I look back at why the football Cardinals weren't
more successful, the whole thing just wasn't put
together well. They just never had enough good players, and it
wasn't well organized. Even though the football Cardinals made
those changes—mostly hiring new coaches—it just didn't work
out.

Now you're going to ask why.

You always look at the top management. It starts with the top
man in any business. You can't avoid the responsibility and the
criticism and the lack of success. With any club I was general
manager of, I was always critical enough to take a sharp look at
myself.

Every owner operates differently. When I was general manager of the baseball Cardinals, Mr. Busch listened to too many out-
siders. That's partly how I was fired twice. Bill Bidwill is his own
man. Good, bad or indifferent, he had his own way of doing
things and he did them. In staff meetings, Bill was always there.
He wasn't overbearing. He would say something on occasion, but
he didn't generally run the meetings. Sullivan ran them. Bill occasionally would talk when they had their meetings on player personnel, but basically he just listened. He might have had opinions
that he expressed on the side, but I never heard that.

He was departmentalized. He delegated authority. He didn't
call the plays from the press box. That would not be Bill Bidwill.
Period. But he had his thoughts; he just kept them to himself until
he needed to make a decision at his level about the head coach or
something like that.

There was an ongoing controversy in St. Louis about Bill
Bidwill's ability to own and operate a successful club. Everybody
criticized him—the fans and media. It became the thing to do.

And from a personal standpoint, Bill never went out of his way to defend himself. When he brought me in, I thought I might be able to help change that. But I couldn't. It became too big for anyone to change. Except the man himself. And the only thing that would change the perceptions was winning.

Recommending Bob Harlan

I had a little more of a positive effect on another pro football team. When I came back to the baseball Cardinals the second time, Dan Devine called me. He had left Mizzou to become the head coach of the Green Bay Packers.

When he called, he said, "I'm going to be the coach and the general manager now. I want to spend most of my time on coaching. So I need somebody to do the paperwork and the detail work on the general manager's side. Can you recommend somebody?"

I said, "Yeah. Bob Harlan."

I had hired Bob to be our public relations director, and I really thought he was good. I liked him even though he was inexperienced, in his early thirties. He had a good work ethic and a good personality.

Devine called during spring training. Bob was already in Florida with the team, and I hadn't gone down yet. But I told Devine how to get in touch with Harlan, and he wound up hiring him.

Bob did a great job in Green Bay. He's another person who is sharp, has opinions, and speaks his mind. He eventually was promoted to team president and chief executive officer. The Packers went to two Super Bowls with Bob Harlan in charge, winning it in '96. He has also expanded their stadium, Lambeau Field, and has the club on sound financial footing.

A HELPING HAND

BOB HARLAN
REFLECTS ON BING DEVINE

When I came to the Cardinals in '65, Bob Howsam was the general manager who hired me. I was in community relations and ran the speakers bureau. Stan Musial was the GM when we won the World Series in '67, and then Bing came in after that.

Jim Toomey was the public relations director, and we heard that he was being promoted to assistant general manager. So I went in to him and said if that was the case, I'd like to be in line for the PR job. Jim talked to Bing, I guess, and it was Bing who promoted me. I worked closely with Bing after that.

Everything with Bing was very businesslike. He was always serious and wanted to hear what your problems were. With Bing, there wasn't a lot of dillydallying to get things done. You went in to see him and you got things wrapped up and you left his office and he went on to something else. I liked that.

The other thing about Bing that I really liked was that he always wanted to deal with something right away. If a problem came up, it was solved the same day—in and out. He'd say, "Let's get at it. Don't let it linger." And that really helped me. If I had a problem, I didn't have to wait several hours to see him. I knew what I would get when I walked in that door. Ten minutes, and I'd be out of there with an answer.

I was the same way. I was young then—in my early thirties—and it gave me confidence to know that the way I liked doing things was the way my boss did, too. I appreciated it then, and I still operate like that. In fact, my wife still says, "I don't dare mention anything to you that needs doing, because you want to do it right now."

I remember that '68 World Series. It was the first time I'd been in the World Series as a PR man. In the '67 Series, Stan was the general manager and I was in a different position with less responsibility. But in the '68 Series, Bing and I spent a lot of time together. I don't remember anything specific coming up. There were no major problems. I just remember that he helped me get through it all very smoothly.

Later on, Bing was the reason I got the job with the Packers. Absolutely. I was at spring training with the baseball club in '71, probably in March. And Bing told me Dan Devine was looking for somebody to handle the paperwork and help with the contracts as assistant GM.

Bing knew I went to Marquette University in Milwaukee and had worked for six years there. So he said, "If you're interested in the Packers, I'll throw your name into the pool."

I said, "I'm not looking to leave, but I'm interested."

So Bing called Dan, and Dan flew down to St. Petersburg and had dinner with Bob Broeg, who was a close friend of his, and me. We had a good talk over dinner, and then Dan flew back to Green Bay. Shortly after that, the Cardinals opened the season in Chicago at Wrigley, say on a Tuesday, and then we didn't play again until Thursday. We had a day off in the middle in case the opener was rained out or snowed out, and my wife flew up to Chicago that day, Wednesday, and met me.

Then we flew up to Green Bay together and met with Dan. We started out at his office, then went over to his place. He was building a house up there and living in a duplex until it was finished. He fixed us some sandwiches and eventually offered me the job. We said we'd think about it.

Then we flew back to Chicago. I stayed with the Cardinals and my wife went back to St. Louis. Shortly after that, we accepted the job. And we've been here ever since. But I wouldn't be here if not for Bing and that connection. Dan Devine didn't know me from anyone. Dan was like a god there in Missouri when he was coaching at Mizzou. I don't think I'd ever met Dan in my six years in St. Louis.

The last time I saw Bing was within the last four years, in spring training at Jupiter, Florida. My wife Madeline and I were out there, and Bing was sitting in a deck chair. We went over and said hi. We had a real nice talk, and when we were leaving, I said,

"Things worked out great for us in Green Bay. But this wouldn't have happened if not for you."

He said, "Yep, yep, you deserved it."

That was it. No big hug. Bing doesn't get real emotional. There was never a coldness—he's just businesslike, all the time. I was fine with that then, and I was fine with that when I worked for him. I know how much he cares about the people who work for him.

I appreciated what he represented. Here's a guy who climbed from the very bottom of the Cardinals organization and went all the way to the top. And what he accomplished, building two teams that played in four World Series in five or six years? Nobody ever did that.

Even after all these years, he's still the same way. He might call me up once a year, usually with a request for tickets to something.

He'll say, "Bob, this is Bing. Can I get a couple Super Bowl tickets?"

I'll say, "Sure. How's the family?"

He'll say, "Good. How's yours?"

I'll say, "Fine."

He'll say, "Good. Take care."

I'll say, "You too."

And boom! He hangs up.

It takes a minute, maybe, to cover the whole subject. That's the way we both are. We're not going to spend a lot of money on long-distance calls, I guarantee you.

Chapter 13

Last At-Bat

Linked with Lou

Of all the deals I've thought of and been a part of, I should have a debt of gratitude to Lou Brock. And I do. Lou made his a great deal with the way he played. It would have been a forgotten deal if not for him. All the other principals in that deal faded away quickly, on both sides.

I take a lot of satisfaction in Brock making the Hall of Fame. He finished with over 3,000 hits, back before the designated hitter made that an easier number to reach. He had the stolen base record. He hit for average.

It would have interested me to see what kind of stolen base record he'd have had if he had been a contact hitter and reached base more frequently. He was a big swinger at the plate, and he did have great power. He hit 149 homers in 18 years—not even 10 a year, but that was good for a leadoff guy. But he also had 1,730 strikeouts, nearly 100 a year, which was a lot for a leadoff guy. At one time, he was listed in the top ten of all time for strikeouts, a

record you don't want to have! That's why I say, what if he had
made better contact and reached base more? Maybe Rickey
Henderson wouldn't have been able to come along and break his
career stolen base record.

Besides being a Hall of Fame player, the other thing I'm proud
of is that there's never anything but good things said about Lou
Brock. He was the subject of fan adulation, and his reputation car-
ried on even after he took his uniform off. And there are good reasons for his reputation. When anyone sees him, he is always well
dressed, well polished, a gentleman in every respect who is always
willing to help his community.

If he wasn't in the public eye to the extent that he was, only
those close to him would realize it, because he doesn't call attention to himself or what he's done. I guess you'd have to say, "He's
the kind of person you'd like to be...and like other people to be."

Through the years we've maintained a relationship and a
friendship. We never did anything beyond the general manager-
player relationship. No business dealings, nothing like that. But I
think we both have respect and appreciation for each other.

Who knows what would have happened if he had stayed in
Chicago? Maybe it all would have happened for him anyway. Who
knows if the Cardinals would have been world champions without
him in '64? Maybe it would have happened for us anyway.

I don't think we've ever sat down and discussed it, but I think
we recognize how our careers were entwined. I hate to be repeti-
tive, but there are a lot of people who made that same impression
on me. Lou Brock as a player. Dick Meyer as a boss. Johnny Keane
as a manager. Mike Dyer as a young executive. People who took a
stand. People you could count on. People you could trust. People
who were loyal.

The Ultimate Compliment

Infrequently, I'll be asked to go somewhere and make a
speech. And I'm usually asked to comment about Brock. I
always say, "So-and-so is a player, but not every player is a *ballplay-*

er." To me, there's a difference. Everybody in the big leagues is a player. A ballplayer is someone who plays every play the way it should be played. Every play, every game. That was Lou Brock. He knew the fine points, which makes him a great ballplayer in all respects.

Ballplayers don't make many mistakes. That means outfielders hitting the relay man. Infielders making the play to the right base. Base runners knowing the appropriate time to run. Hitters late in the game taking the first pitch and making the pitcher work. That was Lou Brock.

And look at the rest of those '64 Cardinals. Bill White was a ballplayer. So were Ken Boyer, Julian Javier, and Dick Groat. And Mike Shannon. And Tim McCarver. And Curt Flood to the extreme. That's the whole lineup. Then you look at the pitchers, and there's Bob Gibson. That's why we won. And why we won again in '67 and again in '68. They were all ballplayers. Their personalities, and the personal touch they all had, is what that puts them above the ordinary in their trades and in their business lives.

Still in the Game

Now I'm back with the Cardinals as a special assignment scout, helping Walt Jocketty if he asks my opinion on something. I remember back in spring training in 2000 they were discussing trading for Jim Edmonds. He was with Anaheim, and some people didn't like him. I remember following Jocketty out into the other room and saying to him, "If you make that Edmonds deal, I think it's a good one and you'll like it. If you don't make the deal, I think you'll live to regret it."

On March 23, 2000, Jocketty acquired Edmonds from Anaheim for Kent Bottenfield and Adam Kennedy. I'm not saying we made that deal because I told Jocketty he'd live to regret it if we didn't. I'm not saying that at all. But I remember thinking, "That's exactly what Bob Kennedy told me when Keith Hernandez wanted so much money after we drafted him." It kind of came full circle there.

Winners

I hate to say this because it sounds self-serving, but every club I worked for made the grade to win fairly quickly after I was hired. That could have been an accident. And maybe it was. But that's the way it was.

I started at Class D ball in the minors at Johnson City in 1941, and we went to the playoffs. I then went to Fresno and we made the playoffs again, but the league folded because of the war. We went to the playoffs in Columbus, Georgia, and won the Sally League title. We were in the playoffs every year I was in Rochester. We even went to the Little World Series twice and won one of them.

With the Cardinals, it took a few years after I was general manager in '57, but we went to the World Series in '64, '67 and '68 and won the first two times. I was with the Mets in '65, '66 and '67, and they won the World Series in '69.

After I left the Cardinals the second time in '78, I went with Montreal, and the Expos made it to the playoffs in '81. I started scouting for Philadelphia from 1988 to 1998, and they went to the World Series in '93. I went to the football Cardinals from 1981 to 1986, and they went to the playoffs in '82 and lost at Green Bay.

I was the first vice president when the St. Louis Sports Commission was formed in 1989, and I served on the board of directors. And that led to a string of successes, like the record-setting 1994 U.S. Olympic Festival and the Men's and Women's Final Four.

I went back to baseball in '99 to scout for the Astros, and they made the playoffs that year. Then I came back to the Cardinals in 2000, and they made the playoffs my first three years.

Maybe it was all a coincidence. And it certainly wasn't just my addition that made the difference. But apparently I contributed something of value, as did many others. This isn't a one-man show.

Maybe I'm just a lucky guy. I know I wasn't a very lucky guy trying to hold a bat! But after that, it all just worked out.

Missing in History

I guess the history books don't really show what I did with the Mets for my three years in New York. I didn't realize that until we started researching some things for this book. Officially, I was only the general manager of the Mets for my last year there. I really made the moves for about three years, though, from '65 to '67. I haven't gotten credit for everything that I did. That's understandable, since technically I was there as the assistant to George Weiss at the beginning. But I don't pay much attention to that. I never even thought about it then, and I never think about it now. When you're there doing your job, you do what you have to do and go on to the next thing.

Who received credit for the '69 Mets? That's ancient history. Whatever history book you're talking about—wars, administration changes, whatever—it probably doesn't cover everything, either. Particularly when you're dealing with personal relationships and personal feelings.

A history book just gives you the sum and substance of what happened. When you get inside of that, there are probably all kinds of additional stories that could be told. When the Mets won in '69, Johnny Murphy was there—and had been there for a number of years. He was the general manager, so that's understandable that he received the credit.

I understand that a lot of things I did are so far gone that it doesn't make an impact on modern-day people. They don't go that far back. So when people ask me if I should be in the Baseball Hall of Fame in Cooperstown, I say, "I don't think so." I don't put a lot of thought into off-the-field people being in Cooperstown. If there are front office people in the Hall of Fame, that's fine. I don't begrudge them that. It's just my opinion that Cooperstown should be reserved for field personnel.

I'm very well satisfied that I'm in the Washington University Hall of Fame in St. Louis, the Rochester Red Wings Hall of Fame in New York, and the Missouri Athletic Hall of Fame in Springfield. I don't even think that I'll ever make it into the

University City Walk of Fame, although I can understand why I might be a good candidate.

But Cooperstown? Forget it.

Taking the Blame

Trading Steve Carlton may not have been my idea, and I may have fought it, but I still take responsibility for that trade. It wasn't like Mr. Busch made me give him away. I had some time to make a deal. And I got Rick Wise, who was a pretty good pitcher then. But I don't want to be the kind of guy who takes credit when something goes right and ducks blame when something goes wrong. I just have a strong inclination against people who do that. That bothers me.

To me, one person on a ball club shouldn't get all the credit for something anyway. The credit one receives in baseball comes from succeeding. And that takes the efforts of the whole ball club, on the field and in the front office.

No Grudges, No Regrets

Some people can't understand why I'm not bitter about being fired the first time, when Branch Rickey was involved and the Cardinals went on to win the pennant and the World Series in '64 without me. Even then, and certainly now, the last thing I want to do is disparage Branch Rickey's memory. And it shouldn't be denigrated. He did so many great things for baseball. Besides, what I experienced is simply life in the fast lane for a general manager. That's what it amounts to. If you want to be an executive or CEO of a company, you've got to take the heat along with the benefits.

Rickey's actions and the issue with Dick Groat might have been contributing factors to my demise, but that's just the way it goes in this job. That's why I didn't dwell on it then, and I don't want to dwell on it now. But I don't think I would have done what he did if our positions were reversed and the opportunity arose. At least my nature wouldn't incline me to do it.

Ringing True

There's something else you should know about Gussie Busch. After I was fired in '64 and the Cardinals went on to win it all, the players voted to chip in and buy me a World Series ring, which I thought was a great gesture. It would have cost them money out of pocket. And it certainly indicates that they had some loyalty to me for putting it all together.

Well, Mr. Busch heard about it. Dick Meyer probably told him. Nothing got past Dick Meyer.

And Mr. Busch said, "No, no, no. Don't do that! Forget about it!"

Which is what you might expect him to say. He had just fired me two months earlier.

But then Mr. Busch said, "The players aren't getting him a ring! We'll put him on the list with everyone else, and the *club* will pay for it."

When Mr. Busch sent that word back to me, again through Dick Meyer, I was very appreciative. Not only that I received a ring, but that it came from the ownership level. It was kind of an apology.

Some owners might have said, "No, you're gone. You don't get a ring."

But that wasn't Mr. Busch. And that tells you something about him. And that's why I mention it now.

Winding Up Rich

People say to me, "Gee, you got fired from a lot of jobs." I say, "Yeah, and I got a lot of jobs!"

But I really was only fired twice, both times by the baseball Cardinals. I left the other ones under my own power. I was the only general manager in big-league history to be fired and re-hired by the same club. I was fired the first time in 1964, in between Executive of the Year awards. I received the award again in 1968, when I came back to St. Louis. The '68 team was the fourth World Series team that I helped to build, and it was the only one I got to watch when I was still the general manager. That was also the only one of the four teams that didn't win the world championship, but that's the way it goes.

As I said, Donald Grant didn't want me to leave the Mets two years before they won it all in '69. He offered me a stake in the club, and I turned him down. I said, "No thank you."

I tell that to people now and they say, "Wow, you're not very smart!"

I think about that now and wonder. What would a small piece of the club mean now? How many millions of dollars would that be worth? Probably a lot. So I guess I'm not smart. But I wanted to be back in St. Louis with my wife and daughters. And as I said to the press at the time:

"They can take me away from the Cardinals, but they can never take the Cardinals away from me."

And now, looking back after all these years, things worked out all right for me and my family.

A MASTER OF EVALUATION

LOU BROCK
REFLECTS ON BING DEVINE

History has uniquely tied us together, Bing Devine and me. The move that he made to trade for me—I imagine that he never knew that it would become his signature piece. I'm kind of glad that it did. I'm a byproduct of that.

I don't even recall the first time we met. After the trade, I joined the team that night in Houston. I didn't talk to Bing then. I was preoccupied with meeting my new teammates. When you don't have a lot of success in your first years in The Show and you get traded, the general manager is not one of the first persons you meet!

When we got back to St. Louis, I did get to talk to him. Again, you're talking about people who obviously knew talent, whether it had manifested itself or not. In my case, there were glimpses of my talent while I was with Chicago, glimpses of greatness, if you want to put it that way. And when you're a "glimpse," you really don't know what will happen, whether you'll just be "glimpses" or rise to the occasion.

But we both wound up with kind of a signature on a small corner of a part of baseball. That's what is unique about the trade, when you look at it. It's been heralded as the worst trade in baseball history—or the second worst. Every year it comes up in that context, when somebody makes a trade that looks lopsided. Many people say the Babe Ruth trade was the worst, but Babe Ruth wasn't traded. He was sold by the Red Sox to the Yankees. So technically, my trade is the worst in the eyes of many people.

I don't talk about the trade. People talk about it. They will ask me about it and then I respond. I know Bing doesn't talk about it either unless somebody asks him. That's what's neat about our history. We all did what we had to do. He did what he had to do in making a trade he thought would help his ball club. I did what I had to do. I performed. That's what happened. But at the time when he was making the deal, none of that had taken place. So it was subject to ridicule. People wondered how he could trade an 18-game winner like Ernie Broglio for a young player who had yet to achieve. And I had the same question: How can they make a deal like that?

But there's one element that's missing here. There's the perception of a player by others, and there's also the perception of a player by himself. As players, we're probably harder on ourselves than the one assessing our ability. We really don't want to go through the process of becoming an outstanding player. It is a process, but we'd rather have it happen overnight. We'd like success to come instantly. We'd rather have a Polaroid snapshot. Unfortunately, it doesn't happen like that. It takes time.

Bing had the ability to sense that. And you know what? Bing's ability to assess a player's ability, that didn't happen overnight either. He had to go through a development process, too. He spent a lot of years in the minor leagues developing his skill, just like players do.

Bing Devine is a man of integrity. People respect him. He's a man of influence, even at his age today. He still has a lot of power and influence in the game of baseball. His evaluation of talent is still intact.

Bing has achieved what he wanted to do. Not many people can say that. He truly did enjoy and love what he was doing.

He's a man who brought his "A" game to the park every day—which is hard to do. Do I admire him? Oh, yeah.

Oh, *yeah*!